JACK THE RIPPER

Discover More of History's Worst

Adolf Hitler

—HISTORY'S WORST—
JACK THE RIPPER

BY **MICHAEL BURGAN**

Aladdin

New York   London   Toronto   Sydney   New Delhi

ALADDIN

An imprint of Simon & Schuster Children's Publishing Division

1230 Avenue of the Americas, New York, New York 10020

First Aladdin paperback edition August 2017

Text copyright © 2017 by Simon & Schuster, Inc.

Cover illustration copyright © 2017 by Matt Rockefeller

Also available in an Aladdin hardcover edition.

All rights reserved, including the right of reproduction in whole or in part in any form.

ALADDIN and related logo are registered trademarks of Simon & Schuster, Inc.

For information about special discounts for bulk purchases, please contact Simon & Schuster Special Sales at 1-866-506-1949 or business@simonandschuster.com.

The Simon & Schuster Speakers Bureau can bring authors to your live event.

For more information or to book an event contact the Simon & Schuster Speakers Bureau at 1-866-248-3049 or visit our website at www.simonspeakers.com.

Cover designed by Laura Lyn DiSiena and Nina Simoneaux

Interior designed by Nina Simoneaux

The text of this book was set in Adobe Caslon Pro.

Manufactured in the United States of America 0717 OFF

2 4 6 8 10 9 7 5 3 1

Library of Congress Cataloging-in-Publication Data

Names: Burgan, Michael, author.

Title: Jack the Ripper / by Michael Burgan.

Description: New York : Aladdin, [2017] | Audience: Age 8–12. |

Includes bibliographical references and index.

Identifiers: LCCN 2017011489 (print) | LCCN 2016043476 (eBook) |

ISBN 9781481479448 (hc) | ISBN 9781481479455 (pbk) |

ISBN 9781481479462 (eBook) |

Subjects: LCSH: Jack, the Ripper—Juvenile literature. |

Serial murders—England—London—History—19th century—Juvenile literature. |

Serial murderers—England—London—History—19th century—Juvenile

literature. | Whitechapel (London, England)—History—Juvenile literature.

Classification: LCC HV6535.G6 L6195 2017 (eBook) | LCC HV6535.G6 (print) |

DDC 364.152/32092—dc23

LC record available at https://lccn.loc.gov/2017011489

CONTENTS

1

THE LAST OF POLLY

The sky glowed red over parts of London's East End on the night of August 30, 1888. Around nine p.m., a fire broke out at a warehouse on the docks along the Thames River, and soon after firemen put that blaze out, another erupted nearby. The second fire burned through the night.

A certain man out walking the streets of Whitechapel, a neighborhood in the East End, would have heard the horse-drawn fire engines racing to the blazes. He would have seen the red sky and perhaps smelled the smoke of the burning buildings. But the fire was not what concerned him that night. He had something else on his mind. He was thinking about murder.

———◆———

POLLY'S NIGHT

MARY ANN NICHOLS must have heard the commotion the fires caused too. She was also walking the streets of Whitechapel that night, though at times she might have stumbled more than she walked. Nichols, who was better known in the neighborhood as Polly, was a heavy drinker—some might say an alcoholic. She was also a prostitute. She often walked the streets at night looking for men who would pay her to have sex with them. Nichols did not make much money this way. But she made enough on the night of August 30 and in the early hours of August 31 to buy drinks in several pubs.

Nichols was not a great beauty. Just five foot two, her hair was turning gray, five of her front teeth were missing, and a scar ran across her forehead. She had turned forty-three just a few days before. Her clothes were shabby—except for the new black hat she proudly wore that night. She had been married once, but she and her husband, William, had divorced eight years before. Nichols left behind five children as she tried to make a life for herself in London.

For a time she stayed at a workhouse. In workhouses across London, the poor and sick lived in crowded dormitories. They worked in return for food and a place to sleep. Women might scrub floors to earn a place in the workhouse, while men might break stones. Anyone who disobeyed a rule or complained about the crowded conditions and bland food would be punished, which could include being whipped.

One of Nichols's last respectable jobs was as a servant. She wrote her father earlier in 1888 that her employers were "very nice people" who lived in "a grand place."[1] But Nichols did not keep the job for long. She stole some clothing and left the house. She sold the clothing, perhaps to buy alcohol.

Nichols ended up in a common lodging house. These houses took in several thousand of the East End's prostitutes and poor working people. Like the others, Nichols paid a daily fee to stay in a tiny room, which she shared. Some lodgers even shared a bed, and each building only had one kitchen. The houses were often called doss houses, as "doss" was street slang for sleeping anywhere one could.

Around twelve thirty a.m. on August 31, Nichols left a pub and headed for a doss house where she had stayed about a week or so before. Yet by now she had run out of money and was turned away. Nichols wasn't worried, though. She believed she could find another customer who would pay her so she could afford a bed. "I'll soon get my doss money," she called out as she went back into the streets.[2]

At about two thirty a.m., Nichols was still drunk and still searching for a customer. Coming up the street she saw a friend, Ellen Holland. She and Nichols had recently shared a room at the doss house Nichols had just left. Holland was returning home after going out to watch the second fire down at the docks. She had seen Nichols drunk a few times before, but she considered her old roommate a nice, quiet person. On this night Holland thought Nichols was too drunk to keep walking the streets, so she asked Nichols to come back with her to the room they once

4

shared. Nichols said no. She headed down Whitechapel Road, determined to find her last customer of the night.

Sometime within the next hour or so, Nichols found her man. She led him onto a side street called Buck's Row. It wasn't unusual for prostitutes to work outside in the darkness if they didn't have money for a room. Nichols and her customer ended up by a row of cottages on a narrow part of the street. Only one of the pair would leave Buck's Row alive.

A GRUESOME DEATH

THE WORKDAY BEGAN early for Charles Cross on August 31. He was a carman—a driver of a horse-drawn carriage. In the years before gasoline-powered cars, horse-drawn carriages, carts, and wagons took people and goods all across London. Some streets also had trams, which carried up to sixty people in cars that horses pulled along rails.

Cross was walking down Buck's Row at about 3:40 a.m. when he noticed something in a gateway across the street. As he crossed the street to inspect the scene, he realized it was the body of a woman. Before he got closer, he heard footsteps down the street. Cross saw another carman, Robert Paul. As Paul approached him, Cross said, "Come and look over here; there is a woman lying on the pavement."

The two men went over to the body. Mary Ann Nichols was lying on her back, with her skirt raised above her legs. Cross took one of her hands; it was cold and lifeless. "I believe she is dead," he said, but when he touched her face, it was warm. Paul put his hand on the woman's heart. "I think she is breathing, but very little if she is," he said.[3] Cross wanted to prop up the body, but Paul pulled away. Cross was now fairly certain that Nichols was dead. He would have known for sure if the morning darkness had not kept him from seeing the deep gash across Nichols's neck.

The two men briefly discussed looking for a **constable**, but neither wanted to take the time, as they were late for work. As they left Buck's Row and entered Baker's Row, they happened to find Constable George Mizen making his rounds. Cross explained what they had found in the dark. Before Mizen could get to the crime scene, Constable John Neil had turned down Buck's Row and found Nichols for himself. He had been down the street just thirty minutes before and not seen a soul. Nichols and her customer-killer either entered the street after he passed, or the darkness had shielded them from his sight. Neil had not heard any screams either, even though his foot patrol never took him that far from Buck's Row.

Using his lantern, Neil inspected the body in the street and saw the slashed throat that Cross had missed. Blood still oozed from the cut. Nichols's vacant eyes stared at the officer, and her new black hat lay by her side. Neil saw Constable John Thain approaching and ordered him to get a doctor. Mizen soon reached the scene as well, and Neil sent him to get an ambulance.

Thain quickly came back to the scene with Dr. Rees Llewellyn, who lived nearby. The doctor saw Nichols's slashed throat and pronounced her dead. Parts of her body, however, were still warm, which told Llewellyn she'd died just a short time before—perhaps only half an hour. And though there was blood around the cut, it was only a small amount. To Llewellyn, this meant Nichols had not killed herself. Someone had murdered her. He told the police to bring her body to the **mortuary**, where he would examine it further.

Before leaving the scene, Neil talked to two men who worked in a nearby slaughterhouse. This part of the East End had several of these businesses, where animals were killed and then cut up to be sold as meat. The men told Neil they had not heard any unusual sounds either.

Constable Thain helped to put the body on the ambulance and noted that the back of Nichols's dress was saturated with blood, which covered his hands.[4] As the ambulance rolled away with Nichols's body, Thain continued to look for clues. He walked around the neighborhood, searching for signs of blood or other evidence. He came up empty-handed.

At the mortuary **Inspector** John Spratling looked over Nichols's body. He pulled up the dead woman's dress high enough to reveal her stomach. He discovered another huge cut that ran from her lower belly up to her breastbone. Through the cut, some of her intestines hung out. Spratling sent for Llewellyn to examine the body again. What he saw astounded him. As he told the newspapers after, "I have seen many horrible cases, but never such a brutal affair as this."[5]

***

THE NEWS SPREADS

LLEWELLYN'S WORDS APPEARED in one of several stories about the killing published in the London papers of September 1. The *Daily News* reported that who had committed the murder and why was "a complete mystery."[6] Yet the paper offered one theory: A gang of men had once terrorized prostitutes in the neighborhood. The gang demanded money. If the women didn't pay, the men threatened to hurt them. The paper also noted that this was not the first terrible murder in Whitechapel in recent months. One had taken place earlier in August, and the *Daily News* suggested that it could have been carried out by the same gang.

News of the Nichols murder crossed the Atlantic Ocean as well. The *New York Times* described the killing in a brief piece labeled "London Crime and Gossip." And the report *was* filled with gossip, as the paper reported a scene that no one else saw or heard: a man running down the street with a knife, chasing a screaming woman whose cries went unanswered. However, the paper's gory description of the victim's body was close to the truth. The *Times* also noted the earlier killings of prostitutes in the East End and said, "The women in Whitechapel are afraid to stir out of their doors unprotected after dark."[7]

Even though Mary Ann Nichols had no papers with her name on her body, the police were soon able to identify her. Some people in the neighborhood heard about the murder and the description of the victim and said the woman seemed to be Nichols. Further proof came when police noted printing on her clothing that had come from the workhouse she had stayed at earlier in the year. Someone from the workhouse came down and positively identified the victim as Nichols. Ellen Holland came to identify the body as well. She cried when she saw her dead friend.

LOOKING FOR MURDER

In nineteenth-century England the process for investigating a suspicious death included a coroner's inquest. The coroner usually had a legal or medical background. He—all were men at the time—was responsible for determining if a death was murder or the result of something else, such as a suicide or accident. After police informed the local coroner of the death, he arranged for a jury to examine the body and hear testimony from witnesses. At the end of the inquest, the jury decided whether or not they thought the death was murder. If they reached a murder verdict, then the police began their formal investigation to look for the killer. Coroners are still part of the legal system in Great Britain, as well as in other countries. In the United States the duties of a coroner are sometimes carried out by a medical examiner. As in London in 1888, some but not all coroners today are also medical doctors. Medical examiners, however, are almost always doctors.

On September 1, Wynne Baxter, the coroner for the Whitechapel area, began his inquest. The witnesses included Nichols's father, her former husband, Ellen Holland, and all the police officers who had seen Nichols's dead body. Dr. Llewellyn offered further details about the condition of the body, including bruises he found on her face. The murder weapon, he thought, was "a long-bladed knife, moderately sharp, and used with great violence."[8] From what the doctor could tell, the person who'd used it to slice Nichols was left-handed. (Later, though, he would admit he couldn't tell for sure, so even this small clue was not helpful.)

Other testimony suggested that Nichols had been murdered at the spot in Buck's Row where her body was found. But no residents who lived close to the scene had heard anything unusual in the street. Somehow the killer had done his gruesome task without his victim making a loud noise of any kind. Then he was able to get away without being noticed. Of course, even if he had blood on his clothes, he would not have been too suspicious in an area with several slaughterhouses. Men often walked the streets with blood-soaked clothes. And once he reached the main street, Whitechapel Road, the murderer could have blended into the crowd. Even at three thirty a.m., the street was already active with people going to work—or prostitutes still doing theirs.

THE VERDICT

WYNNE BAXTER ENDED his inquest on September 22. He summed up for the jury all the evidence and the testimony of the witnesses. As far as a **motive**, he said, "Robbery is out of the question, and there is nothing to suggest jealousy; there could not have been any quarrel, or it would have been heard." He ended by saying, "But one thing is very clear—that a murder of a most atrocious character has been committed."[9]

The jury agreed. In the language used in such inquests, the jury said what happened on the early morning of August 31 was a "willful murder" carried out by "some person or persons unknown."[10]

The murderer, of course, was only unknown to the jury, the police, and the press. Nichols knew who killed her, in the brief time between when he began to slash her body and when she died. But chances are, the last customer she met that night never told her his real name. Somewhere in London only one person knew who had killed her—the man the world soon came to know as Jack the Ripper. And between the morning of August 31 and the end of the inquest, he committed another murder, and more would follow. But the clever Jack left no clues that clearly pointed to who he was. He became and remains the most famous killer who no one has ever identified.

2

A POOR AND CROWDED NEIGHBORHOOD

The Whitechapel neighborhood where Jack the Ripper roamed was one of the poorest in London. It stood in stark contrast to other parts of the city, where wealthy merchants, bankers, and **aristocrats** lived.

London is the capital of the United Kingdom, which is made up of England, Scotland, Wales, and Northern Ireland. The first three of those regions are together called Great Britain. At the time of Mary Ann Nichols's death, Queen Victoria ruled the country, and the 1880s were part of what is sometimes called the Victorian Age. Under Victoria the British built the largest empire of modern times. People sometimes said "The sun never sets on the British Empire," since it spanned the globe. But little of the wealth the British gained from their empire reached the poor of Whitechapel.

Whitechapel sat in the part of the East End that was next to the City of London, which was just one part of the larger area called London. Many centuries before, the City was all of London. A wall around it marked the city limits. Since then, however, London had pushed beyond this original core.

The East End had long been the home of businesses that created stench and filth, such as slaughterhouses and factories that turned fat from animals into tallow. The hard tallow was then used to make such things as candles and soap. The residents of the City did not want such dirty work going on within their walls. Other businesses operated in the area too. During the seventeenth century, French Protestants known as Huguenots settled in the East End neighborhood of Spitalfields. Many worked as weavers or made lace, and as their businesses grew

they built fine homes. Whitechapel also had some fairly well-off residents at the time, but that would change.

IN THE EAST END

DURING THE 1800s, men came to the East End to work on the docks along the Thames River, as British ships arrived with goods from around the world. Some of the workers moved to the city from the English or Irish countryside. Loading large crates of goods on and off ships was not easy, and many men were injured on the job. Still, since so many men were desperate for work, they took what they could get. The shipping companies paid them low wages, knowing they could always find someone else willing to take their place.

As the nineteenth century went on, Great Britain became the world leader in producing such things as cloth and clothing, and new factories in the East End hired workers to produce these and other products. Just as on the docks, working conditions were hard. The factories were hot and dark, and pay was low. Women and children joined men in the factories. Foreign immigrants came to the area too, looking for cheap housing and jobs. In the years before Jack the Ripper began his spree, many of the newcomers were Jewish immigrants from Russia, Germany, and Poland. They came to escape the harsh treatment they often faced in their home-lands because of their faith. Many worked as tailors or shoemakers, as they had before they reached London. Now, though, they often worked long hours—up to twenty per day—for little money.

As more people flocked to the East End, they sometimes struggled to find homes. The fine old Huguenot homes were divided into small apartments, and Spitalfields and Whitechapel were soon known for their crowded, dirty slums. In the slums, many people died from disease or struggled to find enough food to eat. By 1887, about 250,000 people lived in Whitechapel, and perhaps fifteen thousand were homeless. The area's terrible con-ditions could be deadly. About 25 percent of the children there died before the age of five.

Outside the East End, the area around Whitechapel was infamous for the crime that often comes with poverty. One stretch along Commercial Street was called "the evil quarter mile" because of the crime and prostitution that went on there. Some of the problems in the area stemmed from alcohol abuse. Men and women alike tried to forget about the awful lives they faced by drinking too much. Still, one minister in the area said, "The greater part of Whitechapel is as orderly as any part of London."[11] A police detective, however, saw the amount of crime that went on and had a different view. He said that even before Jack the Ripper began haunting the streets, the area had "a reputation for vice and villainy unequalled anywhere else in the British Isles."[12]

Wealthier residents of the city visited the area, a practice that was called slumming. They might come looking for prostitutes or simply to see how awful conditions were. The writer Arthur Morrison came in the spring of 1889 and described seeing "the road sticky with slime" and houses "rotten from chimney to cellar." Many of the women, he wrote, had "sunken, black-rimmed eyes . . . and look so like ill-covered skulls that we start [jump] at their stare."[13]

Some visitors also came hoping to study the conditions of the slums so they could help the people who lived there. One idea was to shut down brothels, houses where several prostitutes worked together, seeing customers. But if a brothel closed in Whitechapel, the prostitutes simply moved on to another neighborhood. In other cases, they began walking the streets in search of customers—as Mary Ann Nichols did the morning she was murdered.

One attempt to improve conditions in Whitechapel started during the 1860s. The city built new housing for the working poor and then tore down some of the worst slums. The new housing, though, was too expensive for most workers, and they had to crowd even more tightly into the cheaper slums that remained. The close quarters, the poverty, the lack of care for the physically and mentally ill—they all combined to create a neighborhood in which crime was common.

———◆———

AN EARLIER MURDER

IN JUNE OF 1887, one year before Jack the Ripper killed Mary Ann Nichols, another Whitechapel murder shook the neighborhood and the entire city. Israel Lipski was a young

Polish Jewish immigrant who made a living making and selling walking sticks. He had two assistants who helped him, but his business was not doing well. Lipski was a border at a lodging house, and another tenant there was Miriam Angel.

One morning when Angel did not come out of her room at her usual time, some people in the house went to see her. Finding the door locked, they broke it down. Angel was lying on the bed—dead. Stains from nitric acid covered parts of her body. In its purest form, the acid can turn metals into liquid, and it's poisonous to humans. Even breathing it can make someone cough up blood. A doctor called to the scene determined she had been dead only a few hours. As he searched the room, the doctor found Lipski lying on the floor, partly under the bed. He was unconscious, but the doctor revived him. Lipski's mouth was also stained with the poison.

For a time Lipski said he had nothing to do with Angel's death. Instead, he claimed he had come to her room and found her dead body, while two men searched for valuables to steal. The men, he assumed, had murdered Angel, and then they beat him and forced some of the acid down his throat—but not enough

21

to kill him. The government, however, rejected Lipski's version of what happened. Instead, they argued in court that Lipski had come to the room to try to have sex with Angel. When she refused, he killed her.

The presence of many poor Jewish immigrants in Whitechapel had led to increased anti-Semitism among some Londoners. Anti-Semitism had a long history in Europe, as some Christians thought Jews were inferior to them. Christians also called Jews "Christ killers" because the Bible describes how they called for the death of Jesus. And some Christians spread the horrible lie that English Jews had once killed Christian babies to use their blood to make a flatbread called matzo. Since Lipski was Jewish, his trial fueled anti-Semitism in London.

Lipski was found guilty and hanged. While a few people thought he had been treated unfairly, Lipski confessed to the murder before his death. He said he only wanted to rob Angel, not have sex with her, and certainly not to murder her. He had bought the poison, he said, to kill himself—which he tried to do after he killed Angel.

Along with increasing the suspicion and hatred of the many

poor Jewish immigrants in the East End, the Angel murder case had another effect. Some people began calling Jews "Lipskis" as an insult. A year after Lipski was hanged, both his name and the hatred of Jews would figure into the hunt for Jack the Ripper.

ANOTHER MURDERER, ANOTHER NEW WORD

The British of the nineteenth century were quick to create new words based on people and events. Decades before "Lipski" became an insult against East End Jews, residents had coined the term "Burking" to describe a particular kind of murder. The word came from the name of William Burke, who, along with his partner in crime William Hare, had killed seventeen people in Edinburgh, Scotland, during the 1820s. The two men learned that Dr. Robert Knox needed dead bodies to conduct medical research—and he would pay for them. Burke and Hare first turned over to Knox a dead body they found in the lodging house Hare owned. Eager for more money and not willing to wait for people to die on their own, the two men began killing others by suffocating them. Their victims included prostitutes. To kill their victims, Burke sat on the person's chest and held his or her nose and mouth shut. Any murder by smothering or suffocation then became known as a Burking. When the two were finally caught, Hare testified against Burke in court. Hare went free, while Burke was executed for his crimes.

———————————————————————

~~~ 3 ~~~

WAS NICHOLS THE FIRST?

Although Israel Lipski's killing of Miriam Angel had been big news the year before Mary Ann Nichols was murdered, a more recent killing had shaken some residents of the East End.

August 6, 1888, was a bank holiday in England. Banks and many other businesses were closed, and some Londoners used the occasion to go to the sea shore or spend the day in the country. For others, the holiday was an excuse to visit pubs and drink.

Martha Tabram and Mary Ann Connelly spent part of that evening doing just that. The two women, both prostitutes, spent several hours in the pubs along Whitechapel Road. During the night they met two soldiers. Around midnight the foursome split off. "Pearly Poll," as Connelly was known, went off with one of the soldiers in one direction. Tabram and the other headed to George Yard, a street not far from Whitechapel Road. George Yard had a series of apartment houses. At eleven p.m. each night, the gas lights outside their stairways went out. The darkness was perfect for Tabram and her customer.

Around three thirty a.m. on the morning of the seventh, Alfred Crow returned to his home in the George Yard Buildings, as the apartments were called. He was a cabdriver and had just finished his work for the night. Entering his building, Crow saw a body on the landing at the bottom of the steps. He couldn't tell if the person was a man or a woman or if the body was alive or dead. Drunk or homeless people sometimes slept on the landing, so Crow ignored the body and went up to bed. But less than two hours later, John Reeves could not ignore the same body when he left his apartment on the way to work. The sun was already beginning to brighten the sky when he saw the body—and the blood that surrounded it.

Unlike Crow, Reeves could tell the person was a woman. And while he did not see a weapon or bloody footprints, he was sure she was dead. Frightened by the scene, Reeves did not stick around to examine the body. He ran out to the street and found a police constable, Thomas Barrett. Soon, a doctor was on the scene. He found thirty-nine stab wounds spread between the victim's throat, chest, and stomach. The doctor guessed she had been dead around three hours, which meant the murder had taken place around two thirty a.m.

WHO WAS SHE? AND WHO DID IT?

THE FIRST BRIEF news reports of the George Yard murder appeared in the paper the next day. But by the start of the inquest on August 9, the police still did not know who the victim was or have any clues. As the *East London Advertiser* noted, "The mysterious nature of the crime, and the utter absence of any clue to the identity of the poor victim, renders the work of the police very difficult and unpromising. We do trust, however, that they may be enabled to get on the track of the brute who has been guilty of such savagery."[14]

Several women came forward to identify the dead body, but each gave police a different name when they said who the victim was. Finally, Henry Tabram saw a news article that gave the woman's last name, and it was the same as his. On August 14, he went to the police and identified the body as Martha Tabram. They were married, though they had not lived together for thirteen years.

At Tabram's inquest, Henry Tabram told of his relationship with the dead woman. The doctor who examined her body, Timothy Killeen, also testified. He said he did not see any signs of struggle before Tabram was murdered. The killer, he said, seemed to have used both a knife and a dagger, which has a different shaped blade than the knife. The killer also seemed to have been right-handed, though one of the wounds might have been made by a left-handed person.

Inspector Edmund Reid was in charge of the case, and he thought one of his own men might have a clue as to who killed

Tabram. On the day her body was found, Constable Barrett told Reid he had seen a soldier in the neighborhood around two a.m. The soldier said he was waiting for a friend who had gone off with a girl. Barrett didn't think anything of this conversation until after the murder was discovered. Could the soldier help Reid find the murderer? Barrett tried to identify the man he had spoken to among a group of soldiers who had been away from their barracks on the morning of August 7. He couldn't spot the man.

Pearly Poll came forward too, detailing the time she had spent with Tabram the night of August 6. She too said she could identify a possible suspect, as she remembered the faces of the two soldiers she and Tabram had spent the evening with. But when she had her chance to identify the two out of a group of soldiers, Pearly Poll said the men weren't there. Shown a different group of soldiers a few days later, she pointed out the two she thought she had seen that night. Both men, however, had alibis. Neither had been near the scene of the crime at the time of the murder.

The investigation seemed to have reached a dead end. Residents of George Yard reported hearing nothing around the time the murder took place. Newspaper reports ended after the second inquest. Martha Tabram might have faded into the history books—if not for the death of Mary Ann Nichols and the eventual appearance of Jack the Ripper. The report of Mary Ann Nichols's murder led several newspapers to connect the two cases, even if there was no evidence to pin down a killer. The *East London Advertiser* wrote on September 8, "There cannot be any doubt that this murder and the previous one . . . were done by the same hand. . . . The cunning of the lunatic, especially of the criminal lunatic, is well-known; but a lunatic of this sort can scarcely remain at large for any length of time in the teeming neighbourhood of Whitechapel." The paper also noted the threat the killer posed to others: "Every woman in those parts goes in nightly danger of her life as long as he remains at large."[15]

MURDER TOURISM

While the brutal killing of Martha Tabram appalled most people, it also stirred curiosity. Some people are drawn to blood and mayhem, and in the days after the Tabram murder, people came to George Yard to see the spot where her body was found. The same thing happened after the death of Mary Ann Nichols, as groups of people visited the site of her murder on Buck's Row. Today several companies in London take as many as a hundred tourists at a time through the streets of Whitechapel, pointing out where Jack the Ripper struck. With such large groups, the tour guides need megaphones to be heard. Their amplified voices upset many of the neighborhood residents. The residents dislike the noise and activity that goes on through the night. One told the *Telegraph* newspaper in 2014, "Imagine if hundreds of strangers were tramping noisily through your backyard every day—would you be happy about it?"[16] The tours are just one example of the continuing fascination with Jack the Ripper and his gory murders.

Despite what the newspapers of 1888 thought, however, today's experts on the Jack the Ripper case argue over whether or not to include Martha Tabram as one of his victims. These experts are sometimes called Ripperologists. Those who think Jack could have been Tabram's killer note that her wounds were in roughly the same area as those of the other victims. And like those victims, Tabram was an East End prostitute. But those who dismiss the idea of Jack as her killer note that Tabram was stabbed, not "ripped" with a knife. And some have argued that even if Constable Barrett and Pearly Poll could not identify a soldier who might have committed the crime, one or more soldiers are still likely suspects. Police investigators who handled the Ripper cases also disagreed on whether Tabram was one of his victims.

But even if Jack the Ripper did not kill Tabram, her death, followed so closely by Nichols's, caused panic in the East End. In September of 1888 the police followed one lead that they hoped would take them to at least one murderer.

A SUSPECT CALLED "LEATHER APRON"

SOME PROSTITUTES OF the East End approached the police with information about a man they knew as "Leather Apron." The women gave him this name because he wore a leather apron for his job—making boots. The police learned that Leather Apron terrorized the prostitutes by demanding money from them. As was the custom of the day, the police did not talk about their investigations with the press. But somehow the *Star* newspaper learned Leather Apron was a suspect. Using its own sources, mostly based on rumor and gossip, the *Star* painted a portrait of a "strange character who prowls about Whitechapel after midnight" and beats up the women who refuse to give him money.[17] Along with his apron, he was known for his sharp knife and his skill at sneaking up on unsuspecting women. The paper also noted that he was Jewish, which only fed the anti-Semitism of the time. It went so far as to call him a "crazy Jew."[18] The *Star*'s reports led many people to think that Leather Apron was the killer of Mary Ann Nichols. It even claimed that he had been seen with her the morning of the murder, which was false.

The police knew Leather Apron's true identity. He was Jack Pizer. They also knew the stories about his treatment of prostitutes. They began to look for him to question him. Pizer, however, was hiding—not from the police as much as other citizens.

He feared that the newspaper reports about him were whipping people into a frenzy. Pizer feared that some might take the law into their own hands and beat him—or worse—if they found him on the streets. The police finally found him on September 10—two days after another brutal Whitechapel murder.

4

A POSSIBLE CLUE,
A DEAD END

On Saturday, September 8, 1888, the *East London Advertiser* reported on the funeral of Jack the Ripper's first definite victim, Mary Ann Nichols. Two days before, several thousand people had lined the streets of Whitechapel as a hearse came to take Nichols's body from the mortuary to the cemetery. Concern about the latest murder, the newspaper reported, was at a "fever heat," and one of the worst things about the killings was that there was no real explanation for them. The paper also suggested that "the murderer must creep out from somewhere; he must patrol the streets in search of his victims. Doubtless he is out night by night . . . and unless a watch of the strictest be kept, the murder of Thursday will certainly be followed by [another]."[19]

As East Enders read those words on Saturday morning, they wouldn't have known how right the newspaper was. In the early hours of that day, Jack had killed again.

———◆———

DARK ANNIE'S TALE

ELIZABETH LONG BEGAN her day on the eighth early, rising before five a.m. to go to the Spitalfields Market. For more than two hundred years, residents of the neighborhood had come to the market to buy fresh produce. Long left her home on Church Street and headed toward Hanbury Street. The sun was approaching the horizon, and the streets were soon busy with other people going to the market. As Long walked she heard a clock chime, marking the half hour. Turning onto Hanbury, she saw a man and a woman talking. The woman was short, plump, and dressed in black, her clothes old and dirty. Long could see the woman's face, which was round, and she had short curly hair. Long could not see the man's face, as his back was turned to her, but she had the sense that he was not English. He was taller than the woman and slightly better dressed, with a dark coat. He wore a brown deerstalker hat—a hat with a visor in both the front and back, and ear flaps that are usually pinned up. Long didn't know it, but the woman was Annie Chapman, and the man she was talking to was almost certainly Jack the Ripper.

Chapman, like both Nichols and Tabram, made at least some of her money working as a prostitute. Her friends knew her as Dark Annie. Almost forty-seven years old and the mother of three children, Chapman and her husband, John, had separated about six years before, largely because of Annie's alcohol abuse. Her husband sent her money until his death in 1886. Chapman then began selling flowers and items that she crocheted, along with her own body. In addition to her other woes, Chapman was suffering from tuberculosis, a lung disease.

Like so many people in Spitalfields and Whitechapel, Chapman lived in a common lodging house—or she had, until she had a fight with another renter. Usually Chapman got along with her neighbors, but starting about ten days before the eighth, she had a running argument with Eliza Cooper, who had loaned Chapman some soap. Nasty words turned to blows, and Cooper left Chapman with a black eye and bruises. A few days later Chapman left the lodging house and did not return until September 7. She visited with friends in the shared kitchen, then left and returned several times, into the early hours of September 8. On at least one trip, she went out for a drink. Around 1:45 a.m. Chapman asked the man who ran the house, Timothy Donovan, to hold a bed for her until she had enough money to pay for it. He said, "You can find money for your beer, and you can't find money for your bed."[20] Like Mary Ann Nichols before her, Chapman went back out onto the street to look for the money she needed.

A BACKYARD MURDER

THE QUEST FOR money for a bed seems to explain why Elizabeth Long saw Chapman with Jack the Ripper on Hanbury Street.

Passing by them, Long heard snatches of the couple's conversation. He said, "Will you?" and Chapman replied, "Yes."[21] Long kept walking to the market, and Chapman and Jack made their way into the backyard of 29 Hanbury Street.

Like many of the buildings in the area, number twenty-nine had once been a fine home. Now it provided cheap rooms to a variety of renters. One of those renters was John Davis, who lived there with his wife and three sons. The family had been at the house just two weeks, but Davis already knew that prostitutes sometimes slipped into the backyard with their clients. Apparently Chapman knew it too.

Davis heard the clock of a nearby church strike 5:45, and he got up to get some tea. After about fifteen minutes he went outside and saw the body of Annie Chapman, her dress pulled up almost to her waist. Davis did not investigate; instead, he ran back into the house, through the front door, and onto the street, calling to three men standing in front of a nearby building. "Men, come here!" the obviously upset Davis yelled to them.[22] The men—James Green, James Kent, and Henry John Holland—went with Davis into the backyard. They quickly realized why he was so upset. Kent noticed a bloodstained handkerchief around Chapman's throat. Blood covered her face and hands as well. Testifying at the inquest the following week, Kent said, "She appeared to have been on her back and fought with her hands to free herself. The hands were turned toward her throat."[23] Kent also saw a ghastly sight: Chapman's intestines and other nearby organs were spilling out of her body.

THE WORST SO FAR

THE THREE MEN went to find a constable. Kent went to his workshop to find something to cover the body. When he returned, Inspector Joseph Chandler was on the scene. In his report he described how Chapman's intestines had been pulled up toward her shoulder, though they were still attached to her body. Her neck, he wrote, was "cut deeply from left and back in a jagged manner right around the throat."[24]

Police surgeon Dr. George Phillips soon arrived. He ordered that the body be sent to the mortuary, then he and Chandler began to inspect the crime scene. Despite all the blood on and around Chapmen, the two men could not find signs of blood elsewhere. This told Phillips the murder had occurred in the backyard. They did, however, find a few small items that they assumed had been in Chapman's pocket: two combs, a piece of muslin fabric, and part of an envelope that held two pills. A postmark showed that the letter had been mailed in London about two weeks before.

When Phillips examined the body, he saw that Chapman's tongue was swollen. That indicated that the killer had partially strangled her. The pressure on the throat and the quick, deep cut around her neck meant that she most likely died before she had a chance to scream for help. Phillips explained all this at the inquest, where he also revealed more details about the wounds to the rest of Chapman's body. The London newspapers thought the facts were too gruesome to reveal. They left out that, along with cutting Chapman open and pulling out her guts, Jack had removed her womb—the part of a woman's body in which babies develop. A magazine for doctors, however, did report the details, and suggested that "obviously the work was that of an expert" or at least someone with enough knowledge of the human body "to secure the pelvic organs with one sweep of a knife."[25]

At the mortuary Timothy Donovan and Chapman's brother, Fountain Smith, identified the body. Elizabeth Long saw it as well and said it was the same woman she had seen on Hanbury Street. The jury at the inquest saw it too, though parts of the body were covered to hide the awful evidence of Jack's "ripping."

———◆———

SEARCHING FOR SUSPECTS

ONE PIECE OF evidence found near Chapman's body briefly set off a frenzy in the East End. In the backyard was a wet leather apron. People of the neighborhood immediately linked it to Joseph "Leather Apron" Pizer, and anti-Semitic feelings took off again. Some of the residents believed that no Englishman could commit such horrible murders, so they looked to the Jews in general and Pizer in particular as suspects. After Pizer was arrested on September 10, he was able to produce witnesses who could defend him. They said they were with Pizer the nights of the

Nichols and Chapman killings, and the police believed them. The police also let Pizer appear under oath at the Chapman inquest, so he could publicly clear his name. The inquest also revealed that the suspicions linking Pizer to Chapman's murder were overblown. The wet leather apron, it turned out, belonged to the son of the landlady at 29 Hanbury Street.

With Pizer cleared, the police once again struggled to find new clues about the killer's identity and why he killed. Almost as soon they found a possible new suspect or a theory to explain the murders, it was shot down. Coroner Wynne Baxter raised the possibility that Chapman's murderer took her womb so he could sell it to medical researchers in either Great Britain or the United States. Baxter said he received word that an unknown American had contacted a museum official in England looking to buy a womb. British doctors, however, quickly dismissed the idea. One said researchers could get that and any other body parts they might need through legal means.

One story that intrigued police came from a pub not far from the Chapman murder scene. The bartender and two customers said they saw a wild-eyed man come into the pub for a beer just a little more than an hour after Chapman's body was found. His shirt was torn and he had blood on his face and hands.

The following night, a man in another pub outside London drew attention to himself. William Piggott loudly talked about hating women. After he was arrested, police found in his belongings a bloodstained shirt. Piggott admitted that he had been in Whitechapel on Saturday, and he said the blood came after he got into an argument with a woman and she bit his hand. London police thought Piggott could be the same man seen in the Spitalfields pub, so they took him to the city. The witnesses there, though, said Piggott was not the man. Through September, the police questioned several other suspects without arresting anyone for the Chapman murder.

In the days after the murder, strange writings appeared on doors and building walls near the murder scene, adding to the neighborhood's fear. One of the most chilling read, THIS IS THE FOURTH. I WILL MURDER 16 MORE AND THEN GIVE MYSELF UP. Walter Dew, a young detective at the time, wrote years later about the Ripper murders. He said of the graffiti near Hanbury Street, "The public, ready by this time to believe anything, assumed that this message and others similar could have been written by the man who inspired their dread." He added, "Far more likely that the writing was the work of mischievous-minded people who obtained some grim pleasure in adding to the fears of an already demented people. Unfortunately, the 'Ripper' messages were read by children as well as adults. Many of them became so nervous that they were afraid to go to school. Jack the Ripper became the children's bogey man."[26]

Meanwhile, concerned citizens of Whitechapel came together to see what they could do to find the killer. Some of them formed the Mile End **Vigilance** Committee. Its members included several Jewish residents who hoped to combat the rising anti-Semitism. On September 11, the committee announced it was raising money so it could offer a reward. The money would go to anyone "who shall give such information that will bring the murderer or murderers to justice."[27] The committee, though, had trouble raising money in the neighborhood, so it wrote to the government, even sending a letter to Queen Victoria. The government, however, was not interested in offering a reward.

As September went on, the fear that gripped the East

End after the Chapman murder faded a bit. And the *East End Advertiser* reflected some of the frustration some people must have felt as rumors and false clues emerged. Writing about the alleged clues, the newspaper wrote, "One had got almost weary of a word so often abused by being made to stand for what meant nothing and led nowhere."[28] So with the police having no leads or solid evidence, Jack the Ripper was still free to roam the streets.

FINDING THE FACTS

Over the decades since Jack the Ripper terrorized Whitechapel, various students of the case have spread false tales about the details of the Annie Chapman murder. At least that's the view of respected Ripperologist Philip Sugden. In his book *The Complete History of Jack the Ripper*, he pointed out some of the myths—and highlighted why understanding the truth about the Ripper murders is often difficult. In some cases, other writers misread the original texts on the case, such as the inquest reports and newspaper accounts. That led to one writer saying Jack had removed Chapman's kidney, which never happened. One of the most outrageous stories involves the handkerchief that was tied around Chapman's neck. False newspaper reports of 1888 said that the murderer had tied the cloth around her neck to keep her head on her body after he nearly cut it off. The evidence given at the inquest clearly showed that Chapman was wearing the handkerchief before she met Jack, and the wound to her throat was not that severe—though grisly enough. The handkerchief story still appeared in some books almost one hundred years after the killing.

5

HAS JACK BEEN SPOTTED?

Through most of September, other killings happened in the East End, but none fit the pattern established in the earlier bloody murders. A murder outside the city, however, in rural Birtley, drew some attention. The body of Jane Beadmore was found near a railway with knife wounds to the face and stomach. Several papers immediately drew a connection to the Whitechapel murders. The *Pall Mall Gazette* reported on

September 24, "In some respects the [Birtley] murder is said to closely resemble them; and already the people in the neighborhood have begun, it seems, to be haunted with the idea that the murderous maniac of Whitechapel may have made his way to the North of England. The idea is natural, but improbable. What is far more likely [is] that the Birtley murder is not a repetition, but a reflex, of the Whitechapel ones. It is one of the inevitable results of publicity to spread an epidemic. Just as the news of one suicide often leads to another, so the publication of the details of one murder often leads to their repetition in another murder."[29]

Police in Birtley began to suspect William Waddell of the murder. He had disappeared after the killing. He had once been in a relationship with Beadmore and was known to have taken an interest in the Ripper slayings. Waddell was arrested and finally admitted his crime, saying that he was probably drunk or crazy at the time. He also seemed to confirm what the *Gazette* had suggested, saying, "that he had been reading the accounts of the murders in London."[30]

OUT ON A RAINY NIGHT

NEWS OF THE Beadmore killing appeared in the London papers for several days, but after September 29 the attention turned back to Whitechapel. That evening Elizabeth Stride left her doss house at 32 Flower and Dean Street, east of Commercial Street. Her friends called her Long Liz, though she was only a little over five feet tall. Stride earned money in various ways, including prostitution. She seemed to spend a good bit of what she made on alcohol, as she had been arrested a few times for being drunk and disorderly. On the twenty-ninth, Stride made some money cleaning two rooms in her lodging house, and she had the money with her when she left the house around seven p.m.

By one account, two men saw Stride about four hours later with a man. From inside the pub, J. Best and John Gardner saw the couple hugging and kissing in the doorway. Stride and her friend had been inside drinking. They seemed ready to leave, but since it was a rainy night they lingered in the doorway. Best later said, "He seemed a respectably dressed man, [and] we were rather astonished at the way he was going on with the woman, who was poorly dressed. . . . I said to him 'Why don't you bring the woman in and treat her?' but he made no answer." To the woman, Best joked, "That's Leather Apron getting round you."[31] Best was sure the man was English, and he said he had a black moustache. After a few minutes in the doorway, the couple took off.

About ninety minutes later, Constable William Smith saw Stride and a man—perhaps the same one, perhaps not. Smith was making his rounds on Berner Street, several blocks south of the pub. Smith thought the man was respectably dressed, and he had a moustache. He also wore a dark deerstalker cap, as had the man Elizabeth Long saw before the Annie Chapman murder. Smith could not hear the couple talk, but he noticed that Stride had a red flower in her jacket, and the man carried a small package wrapped in newspaper. Seeing nothing suspicious, Smith continued his rounds.

Smith had seen Stride and the man outside a courtyard called Dutfield's Yard. The buildings along the yard included the home of the International Working Men's Education Club. Its members were Socialists—they opposed the private ownership of businesses and wanted more rights for workers. Men came to the club for political discussions and to socialize. Most of the members were Jewish immigrants from Germany and Poland.

JACK STRIKES AGAIN

ONE OF THE members was Morris Eagle. He had come to the club for its weekly Saturday evening lecture, left to bring home a friend, then returned about 12:40 a.m. He didn't notice anything in the yard. But just twenty minutes later, Louis Diemschutz did. He entered the yard in a small horse-drawn wagon. The horse saw something to the right that seemed to spook him. Diemschutz looked over and saw a shape in the dark. Climbing off the wagon, he lit a match that gave him just enough light to see a woman's body.

Diemschutz went into the club and called out that there was a woman lying in the yard, "though I could not say whether she was drunk or dead."[32] He then went back into the yard with a candle and saw blood near the body.

Diemschutz and another man ran to find a constable. They couldn't see one, but another man they met on the street joined them as they returned to the scene of the crime. This man, Edward Spooner, knelt down and lifted the woman's head a bit—enough for Diemschutz to see the cut there. Blood flowed from a wound over two inches wide.

Soon after, Morris Eagle located a constable, and Dr. Frederick Blackwell arrived on the scene around 1:15 a.m. He saw the huge gash in the throat but didn't notice any blood on the woman's clothes. The cut, he noticed, had sliced her windpipe in two. Blackwell guessed the woman had died about thirty minutes before he arrived. Another doctor who examined her said the murder could have occurred as early as 12:36 a.m. In either case, Diemschutz had spotted the body very soon after the killing. Police closed the gate to the courtyard and questioned everyone in it. This included some people who lived in cottages in the courtyard and members of the International Working Men's Education Club. The doctors looked them over for bloodstains but found nothing. Once again, the police were dealing with a murder that had no solid clues or suspects.

SEARCHING FOR ANSWERS

THE BODY IN Dutfield's Yard was Elizabeth Stride, though it would take police several days to confirm her identity. At the mortuary Inspector Edmund Reid examined the body. He saw the red flower still in her jacket, the one Constable Smith had spotted.

The hunt to identify Stride became harder when Mary Malcolm showed up and insisted the victim was her sister Elizabeth Watts, who lived in the doss houses of the East End. Malcolm even swore under oath that the dead woman was her sister. Malcolm, it turned out, was wrong, because her sister was alive, and she accused Malcolm of deliberately lying about her.

The police finally identified Stride as the victim. She was a Swedish immigrant who had begun working as a prostitute before coming to England. In her new home she married a carpenter, but the marriage didn't last. Elizabeth Stride spent time in workhouses and accepted charity from a Swedish church in London. She also met a man named Michael Kidney and spent some time living with him, though she often left him when she had too much to drink.

Even before the inquest revealed anything about Stride, police received a statement from a man who thought he might have seen the murderer. On the evening of September 30, Israel Schwartz told his story at the Leman Street Police Station. Chief Inspector Donald Swanson later summarized Schwartz's statement. Schwartz said he was walking down Berner Street and saw a woman in the gateway at Dutfield's Yard. Then a man stopped and spoke to the woman. As Swanson recounted it, "The man tried to pull the woman into the street, but he turned her round and threw her down on the footway, and the woman screamed three times but not very loudly."[33] Schwartz then crossed the street and noticed a man on that side lighting a pipe. The man with the woman called out, "Lipski," and Schwartz began to walk away. As he did, the man with the pipe began to follow him, so Schwartz broke into a run and the man stopped tailing him. Schwartz told police he couldn't say for sure if the two men were somehow working together. But when he saw Stride's body in the mortuary, he said it was the woman he had seen in the gateway. Schwartz said the first man was medium height and had a moustache.

While Inspector Swanson believed Schwartz's version of the events, the witness was not called to speak at the inquest, and no one knows why. But for the first time, the police had some indication, if only slight, that Jack the Ripper might not work alone.

The *Star* newspaper somehow learned about Schwartz's visit to the police station and offered its own version of his story. It claimed that Schwartz had seen the second man come out of a pub and begin "shouting some kind of warning to the man who was with the woman," before the second man began chasing after Schwartz with a knife.[34] The newspaper article might have made the scene more dramatic than it really was, as the papers sometimes did with the Ripper murders. But in general it was similar to Inspector Swanson's account. The paper also noted that Schwartz spoke very poor English, but he would have had no trouble understanding the name Lipski.

Still, no one could be sure if Schwartz was telling the truth or if he had really seen Stride with the man who killed her. At the inquest one constable reported that he had seen various arguments taking place around Berner Street near the time of the murder. Schwartz might have seen one of these. Ripperologists have also wondered about Schwartz's claim that Stride's attacker called out "Lipski." Some British government officials thought that Lipski was the second man's name and that both unknown men were Jews. But the attacker could have been referring to Schwartz, who was Jewish, using the name many English people commonly used at the time for any Jew in the East End. In any event, when police questioned the residents of the area, nobody knew of a Lipski who lived nearby.

COULD JACK BE AMERICAN?

In both the Chapman and Stride cases, small details emerged that raised the possibility that Jack the Ripper came from the United States. With Chapman, coroner Wynne Baxter said the bizarre request seeking women's body parts came from an American. In the Stride case, shopkeeper Matthew Packer of Berner Street claimed that he sold grapes to her and a man with her about an hour before the killings. He said the man wore a "kind of Yankee hat," using a word many English would use for someone or something American.[35] Later, Packer told a reporter that the man spoke with a Yankee accent. Packer, like Schwartz, identified Stride in the mortuary as the woman he saw that night. But his changing statements to investigators and reporters suggest he was not the most trustworthy witness. The issue of Jack's possibly being American came up again later, as we shall see.

As with the other cases, Stride's death presented questions. Unlike Annie Chapman and Mary Ann Nichols, Stride was not obviously strangled and she did not have the ripping wounds in her stomach. But the cut to her throat was similar to the others, and like the others Stride was a prostitute killed on a dark and quiet East End street. To most police investigators of that day and Ripperologists of today, Jack had killed Stride. And he was busy on the early morning of September 30, leaving Berner Street to strike again.

6

A BUSY MORNING

September 29 was not a good night for Catherine Eddowes. By eight thirty p.m. she was so drunk that she had fallen down in Aldgate High Street, west of Commercial Street in the East End. Once down on the ground, she couldn't get up. A crowd gathered around her, drawing the attention of Constable Louis Robinson. The officer asked if anyone knew the woman, but no one did. Robinson tried to prop up Eddowes against a building, but she slid back down to the street.

She reeked of alcohol. Robinson called another constable to help, and together they brought Eddowes to the nearest police station.

To her friends, Eddowes was better known as Kate Conway. The last name came from a man she had lived with years before, Thomas Conway. They never married but had three children together. After leaving Conway, Eddowes spent many years with John Kelly, with the pair living together at a doss house on Flower and Dean Street. They struggled to find enough money to live, doing whatever jobs they could find.

Like many poor Londoners, they traveled out to the countryside in the fall to make money picking hops, a key ingredient in beer. Eddowes and Kelly had made such a trip the day before, but they quickly spent what they had earned. On either the evening of the twenty-eighth or the morning of the twenty-ninth, Kelly offered to pawn his boots. That meant taking the boots to a pawnshop, which would give him money for them. Kelly would have to repay the money later, plus a little extra, if he wanted the boots back. Eddowes took the boots to the shop and got enough money for them to eat breakfast. In the afternoon the pair left the doss house, each going to look for money.

Despite the couple's hard finances, Kelly and others who knew Eddowes said she never worked as a prostitute, though some modern Ripperologists dispute this. But she was known to drink too much alcohol. And she obviously found enough money that day to buy the liquor that left her passed out on Aldgate High Street. Before she and Kelly had gone their separate ways that day, he told her to be careful, reminding her of the Whitechapel murders. "Don't you fear for me," Eddowes replied. "I'll take care of myself and shan't fall into his hands."[36]

❖

FROM JAIL TO MITRE SQUARE

AFTER HER DRINKING bout and arrest, Eddowes found herself in the Bishopgate Police Station. The officer in charge asked for her name. "Nothing," she replied. An officer then led her to a cell so she could sleep off the effects of the alcohol. Around twelve thirty a.m., Constable George Hutt checked on her to see if she could be released. Eddowes asked when she would be freed. She said, "I am capable of taking care of myself now."[37] Within half an hour, the officer in charge said she could go, and Hutt escorted her out of the station. Before she left, Eddowes asked him what time it was. "Too late for you to get any more drink," he said, and then he told her the time. Eddowes realized that Kelly would not be happy when she got home so late. She then said good night and left the station. At almost the same time, in another part of the East End, Louis Diemschutz found Elizabeth Stride's body at Dutfield's Yard.

About forty-five minutes later, Constable Edward Watkins was making his rounds. He entered Mitre Square, a small square just four hundred yards from the Bishopgate Police Station and within the boundaries of the City of London. The square was lined with warehouses and just a few homes, and only two streetlamps offered any light. When he'd passed this way around one thirty, Watkins had found the square empty. But this time, as he turned to the right, the beam from the lantern attached to his belt fell on something. In the darkest part of the square, he saw a woman lying on her back in a pool of blood. Her clothes were up to her waist, her throat was slit, and her stomach was cut open. Later Watkins told the *Star* that the woman was "ripped up like a pig in the market." He had been an officer for seventeen years, but he said, "I never saw such a sight."[38] From what he knew of the recent Whitechapel murders, Watkins realized that Jack the Ripper had struck again.

Watkins ran into one of the nearby warehouses and found a night watchman on duty. "For God's sake, mate, come to my assistance," Watkins said. "Here is another woman cut to pieces."[39] The watchman, George Morris, grabbed his lantern and followed Watkins into the square. After a quick look at the body, Morris ran into the street to find more officers. By two a.m., several officers and a doctor were on the scene. The doctor determined that the woman had been dead only fifteen minutes or so. Soon after, police doctor Frederick Gordon Brown arrived and more thoroughly examined the woman. Though it would take several days to identify the victim, it was Catherine Eddowes.

ANOTHER GRUESOME DEATH

ON OCTOBER 1, the London newspapers reported on the two new Whitechapel murders. The *Daily News* noted the similarities between Eddowes's mutilated body and Annie Chapman's. As with that victim, Jack the Ripper had pulled Eddowes's intestines out of her body and draped them over her shoulder. He'd also removed her womb. But this time, Jack had gone even further in his sick work. He'd cut part of the intestine off and placed it beside the body. He'd removed Eddowes's left kidney. Eddowes also had part of her right ear and the tip of her nose sliced off, and there were other cuts to her ear and face unlike any of the other victims. But for all his ripping, Jack had left behind almost no traces of blood on Eddowes's body below her stomach or signs of spurting blood on the pavement.

A few days later at the inquest, Dr. Brown spelled out all these gruesome details. Coroner S. F. Langham asked if the killer had any special knowledge of the human body. Brown replied, "He must have had a good deal of knowledge as to the position of the abdominal organs, and the way to remove them." Removing a kidney, he said, was especially tricky, "because it is apt to be overlooked, being covered by a **membrane**." Brown also said that someone used to cutting up animals could also have this knowledge. Then, when asked if he had an opinion why someone might remove the body parts, Brown simply said, "I cannot give any reason whatever."[40]

The day after the twin killings, the *Daily News* reported the police's suspicion that Jack had been scared off for some reason after killing Elizabeth Stride and "so made off in the direction of the City with the ghoulish thirst for blood still blazing within him; that he beguiled another hapless victim into a dark secluded spot, and then again fell to his butchery."[41]

Later that day the *Evening News* reported that a clue had been found in a doorway on nearby Goulston Street: a piece of cloth that came from a torn apron found near Eddowes's body. Several other policemen had gone by the doorway earlier, after Eddowes's murder, but they had not seen the scrap of cloth. That suggested that Jack had been in the neighborhood for up to an hour after the killing, eluding the police already questioning anyone they met. He must have dropped the piece of apron in the doorway after those two officers passed by.

The fragment of the apron looked like a bloody knife had been wiped on it. The apron seemed like the first real clue that Jack had left behind. What the newspaper didn't know about, however, was the writing found on the wall near the doorway. It read: "The Juwes are the men that will not be blamed for nothing."[42]

THE MYSTERY OF THE GRAFFITI

THE OFFICER WHO found the strange message written in chalk belonged to the Metropolitan Police, which handled crimes committed outside the City of London. The previous Ripper murders had all taken place outside the small area that defined the City. Eddowes, though, had been killed in the City, although close to Whitechapel. The City of London had its own police force, so now two different police forces were investigating murders that appeared to have been committed by the same person. And when it came to the graffiti, they didn't agree on how to handle it.

The writing was discovered in a largely Jewish neighborhood. Even though the graffiti misspelled the word "Jews," some Metropolitan officers feared it might upset the area residents or lead to more anti-Semitism in the area. City police officers, meanwhile, wanted the writing photographed as evidence. But before that could happen, Thomas Arnold, a high-ranking official on the Metropolitan Police force, ordered that the chalk writing be washed away. As he later explained, because of the attention given earlier to John "Leather Apron" Pizer and the anger the Chapman murder stirred against Jews, Arnold feared a riot could have broken out after people saw the writing the next day.

Sir Charles Warren, **commissioner** of the Metropolitan Police, supported Arnold's decision. He wrote later that leaving the writing up might have led to "an onslaught upon the Jews, property would have been wrecked, and lives would probably have been lost."[43]

At the scene Warren argued with a City detective who wanted to keep the writing on the wall until it could be photographed. Or, as a compromise, the Metropolitan Police could erase "The Juwes are" and leave the rest. Warren, however, insisted that all the graffiti be erased immediately.

Even after it was erased, the graffiti posed several questions with no sure answers. Had Jack written it? Some officers did not think he would stop to write something on a wall when the police were already spreading out through the neighborhood searching for him. Others, though, felt it likely that Jack had written it. So if he did, why? One theory was to try to make people believe the killer was Jewish, as many East End Londoners already did. Still others thought that Jack was Jewish and for some unknown reason had drawn attention to himself and other Jews with the message. That seemed less plausible after a rabbi explained that Jews would not usually refer to themselves as "Juwes." Warren and other officials believed the former theory—Jack wanted to make others think the killer was Jewish and keep police attention away from him.

PHOTOGRAPHING THE RIPPER MURDERS

By 1888, cameras were becoming more common in police work, though they were big and bulky and took time to set up. In 1869, French police had taken what might have been the first pictures of crime victims, photographing several dead bodies at a mortuary just hours after the murders happened. With the Jack the Ripper case, however, the different police forces investigating the murders did not take many photos—or at least not many that survived. Coroners did take mortuary photos of the victims. Some of them show just a head, while one of Catherine Eddowes shows her entire body. But with one exception, police did not take pictures of the victims at the crime scene—most likely because the dead women were discovered at night or near daybreak. If City of London police had photographed the graffiti on Goulston Street, it might have been one of the few pictures showing evidence from the case. The police photos were not meant for public use, though one of Eddowes was published a little more than a decade after her murder. Most have been published since then. During the 1960s City of London police officer Donald Rumbelow found four original mortuary pictures of Eddowes. (He has since become a highly respected Ripperologist.) The City of London Police Museum also has a photo showing part of some other graffiti that was supposedly signed by Jack the Ripper. It reads, "I am going to do one on the 27th."[44] There is no record in the police files about where or when the picture was taken.

A WITNESS AND AN IDENTIFICATION

ALONG WITH STOPPING people on the streets near Mitre Square to look for blood and ask questions, the police knocked on doors in the neighborhood. One local resident who might have seen something was Joseph Lawende, along with his friends Joseph Levy and Harry Harris. The three had spent the night of September 29 at a local club and left for home about one thirty a.m. Near a street that led to Mitre Square, the three men spotted a couple. The man was taller than the woman and had a moustache. She wore a black jacket and a bonnet, just as Eddowes had. Lawende saw the woman put her hand on the man's chest, but he could not see her face. Of the three, Lawende had come to the closest to the couple, yet he told the inquest he doubted he would recognize the man if he saw him again. But given a chance to see the clothes Eddowes wore that night, Lawende said they were the ones he saw.

Until October 2, the police did not know the name of the

Mitre Square victim. But John Kelly, after reading newspaper accounts of the murder, realized she was Catherine Eddowes. The woman had a crude tattoo of the letters *TC* on her left arm. Some time before, she'd told Kelly that her former partner, Thomas Conway, had put the tattoo of his initials there. After the murder, in an article in the *Star*, Kelly read that the victim had the same tattoo. "Man, you could have knocked me down with a feather," he told the *Star* in a later interview. He knew that "it was my Kate, and no other." Kelly identified her for the police.[45]

Even before Kelly identified Eddowes, the City of London took a step that the government had not in the earlier cases. The City offered a reward for any information that led to the killer's arrest and conviction. The British government, though, still refused repeated requests to offer a reward, and even returned money people sent to be used for one. The government stuck by its policy of not offering any rewards for information, as they rarely led to good evidence and produced lots of false clues.

Reward or no, emotions ran high throughout London.

Some people criticized the skills of the police. Others admitted that Jack had been clever in not leaving clues. But perhaps one important clue had appeared before the killings of Elizabeth Stride and Catherine Eddowes. It wasn't found at a crime scene; instead, it came through the mail.

7

"JACK THE RIPPER" IS BORN

The hunt for the Whitechapel murderer wasn't limited to the various police detectives assigned to the case. Amateur sleuths tried to track down Jack as well. Before the Stride-Eddowes double murders of September 30, two men who each suspected the other of being the killer began trailing each other when they could. One day the men finally shared their suspicions with a constable, who brought both of them to the police station. The detectives there got a good laugh listening to the two men's stories before sending them on their way.

Some people turned to the spirit world for guidance. Spiritualism, the belief that the living could contact the spirits of the dead, was somewhat popular in both the United States and Great Britain during the last decades of the nineteenth century. Believers held meetings called séances to try to communicate with the spirits around them. A spiritualist in Cardiff, Wales, claimed to have learned the name and address of the killer. Another in Bolton, England, reported she clearly saw Jack. As the *East London Advertiser* reported, "He wears a dark moustache and bears scars behind the ear and in other places. He will, says the medium, be caught in the act of committing another murder."[46]

People who thought they had clues or knew a possible suspect also wrote letters to the police and the newspapers. For a time, London police received an average of a thousand letters every week on the murders. Most were not published or answered. One woman wrote that the murderer wasn't human—he was actually a large ape that, after killing, "return[ed] home to lock itself up in its cage."[47] Another writer thought the actor currently starring in a play of *Dr. Jekyll and Mr. Hyde* was the killer. The writer claimed that the actor got so worked up playing the murderous Mr. Hyde that he carried the awful emotions with him when he left the stage. Others suggested that some native people from the British colony of India were in London seeking wombs as part of a religious ceremony.

CONNECTING JACK WITH MR. HYDE

In 1886, Robert Louis Stevenson wrote *Strange Case of Dr. Jekyll and Mr. Hyde*. The short novel tells the story of a doctor who creates a potion that turns him into the hideous Hyde. As Mr. Hyde, he enjoys unnamed pleasures that respectable people of the time would have found immoral—perhaps including hiring prostitutes. Hyde also murders a man for no reason. Stevenson's book was immensely popular, and stage versions quickly appeared. The most popular opened in London in August of 1888, just a few days before possible Ripper victim Martha Tabram was murdered. When Mary Ann Nichols was killed at the end of the month, some newspapers made a connection between the murder and the

Jekyll and Hyde play. Could Hyde's actions on stage have somehow inspired a real-life murderer? Some people even referred to the killer as Mr. Hyde. Some people also wondered if the East End killer was like Dr. Jekyll—a respectable, wealthy man who kept hidden his murderous side. The show's producer and star, Richard Mansfield, closed his production of *Jekyll and Hyde* before the double murders of September 30. Some people have suggested he felt pressure to do so because of the earlier murders and how some people tied them to his play. But that seems unlikely, as within a few weeks Mansfield was back on stage playing Dr. Jekyll and Mr. Hyde again.

Some people wrote about dreams they had indicating who the killer was and where he could be found. Others offered suggestions for how to catch the killer. These included giving guns to East End prostitutes or setting up an electric warning system along the streets, with panic buttons about thirty feet apart. A woman facing an attack could push the button, which would set off an alarm in nearby shops. Another plan described in a letter called for using dummies that looked like young women. Their arms and legs would be metal springs that activated when the killer touched the dummy and trapped him until the police could arrive.

JACK WRITES?

AS CRAZY AS some of these letters might have seemed, the Metropolitan Police took particular interest in one they received on September 29. The Central News Agency passed along the letter, which was dated September 25 and had been postmarked two days later. The agency wrote news stories for other papers to use. It was known for writing articles that distorted the facts to make the stories more interesting to readers. In this case, though, the editor at the agency thought the letter was a hoax and didn't publish it. Instead, he sent it to Scotland Yard, the headquarters of the Metropolitan Police (the name also refers to that police force itself). Detectives there didn't think much of the letter either—until the murders of Stride and Eddowes.

Then, the day after those killings, the Central News Agency received and gave to the police a postcard. The two writings made detectives strongly consider the possibility that both had come from the killer.

The letter was dated the twenty-fifth and was written in red ink. It said:

Dear Boss,

I keep on hearing the police have caught me but they won't fix me just yet. I have laughed when they look so clever and talk about being on the right track. That joke about Leather apron gave me real fits. I am down on whores [prostitutes] and shant quit ripping them till I do get buckled [arrested]. Grand work the last job was, I gave the lady no time to squeal How can they catch me now, I love my work and want to start again. you will soon hear of me with my funny little games. I saved some of the proper red stuff in a ginger beer bottle over the last job to write with but it went thick like glue and I cant use it. Red ink is fit enough I hope ha. ha. The next job I do I shall clip the lady s ears off and send to the police officers just for jolly wouldnt you. Keep this letter back till I do a bit more work then give it out straight. My knife's so nice and sharp I want to get to work right away if I get a chance, good luck.

Written sideways below the main letter was another message:

wasn't good enough to post this before I got all the red ink off my hands curse it.
No luck yet. They say I'm a doctor now ha ha

The letter was signed:

yours truly,
Jack the Ripper
Dont mind me giving the trade name

For the first time, the Whitechapel murderer had a name—one that would live on long past the murders stopped.

Several points in the letter caught the attention of the Metropolitan Police. The writer seemed to predict a new murder—or murders—would take place when he wrote, "I love my work and want to start again. you will soon hear of me with my funny little games." More specifically, the letter referred to cutting a victim's ear off, and Catherine Eddowes was the first victim to have cuts on her ear.

The postcard of October 1 seemed even more ominous. The bloodstained card had the same handwriting as the letter and talked about the two murders that had just taken place. Someone playing a sick joke might have had time to read about the killings in the paper and send the card. But in the card the writer talked about not having much time with one victim—which seemed to be the case for Jack with Elizabeth Stride. Taken with the letter, the police thought they might have a solid lead.

TRACKING JACK THE RIPPER

THE NAME JACK the Ripper was soon known all over London, as newspapers reported on the letter and card. The police also put copies of them on posters, hoping someone in the city might recognize the handwriting. As more people heard the name, more letters arrived signed by Jack the Ripper, though none of these seemed authentic. At the time the police thought only the first two they received with Jack's name could be real—an idea some officers believed for some time. But years after the Ripper murders stopped, it seemed that even those letters were probably a hoax. Two high-ranking police officials stated their belief that the writer was a London journalist. Ripperologists today usually identify him as Thomas J. Bulling, a reporter at the Central News Agency. But in October of 1888, the letter and the postcard seemed to be the only real clue.

One more letter drew the police's attention—mostly because of what came with it. On October 16, George Lusk received a package in the mail. Lusk had taken over the leadership of the Mile End Vigilance Committee. The package contained a letter—and half of a human kidney. The note, which was not signed by Jack the Ripper, read:

From hell
Mr Lusk
Sor

I send you half the
Kidne I took from one women
prasarved it for you tother piece I
fried and ate it was very nise. I
may send you the bloody knif that
took it out if you only wate a whil
longer
Signed catch me when
you can
Mishter Lusk

Since taking over as head of the committee, Lusk had received many odd letters, and at first he almost wrote this off as a hoax. He assumed the kidney had come from an animal. But when he went to a committee meeting the next night and mentioned the package, Lusk seemed upset by it. One committee member laughed as Lusk mentioned the letter and the kidney. "It is no laughing matter to me," Lusk said.[48] Some committee members suggested they stop by Lusk's house the next day to examine the package. When they arrived, Lusk gave them a small box that contained the kidney, with the organ releasing a foul smell. The members suggested they bring the kidney to a doctor.

The newspapers learned about the new clue in the Ripper murders, and once again false reports and rumors emerged. The doctor who first examined it said it was human and was from the left kidney—just like the one that had been removed from Eddowes. But the doctor couldn't say if the victim was male or female or how long it had been since the kidney was removed. That didn't stop at least one press report that claimed the kidney was from a woman and that it had been removed around the time Eddowes was killed.

The kidney next went to the Metropolitan Police, who then passed it on to the City of London police for another medical examination. The severed kidney showed signs of a kidney disorder called Bright's disease. Eddowes's remaining kidney did as well. Plus, the mailed kidney had been placed in a liquid to preserve it soon after it was removed. In most murder investigations, the body is not dissected until at least a day after the crime takes place. The kidney had not come from a body that went through that usual process.

Even with that evidence, however, the police couldn't rule

out that the kidney was part of a hoax. And various detectives remained divided in their opinions on whether or not the real killer had sent that package or the Jack the Ripper letters. In the meantime, the hunt for Jack went on.

CALL IN THE BLOODHOUNDS

Early in the Jack the Ripper murders and again after the double killings of September 30, some people suggested that police should use bloodhounds to track the killer. Edwin Brough, who bred bloodhounds, assured readers of the *Times* that "The great value of the pure bloodhound is that he can be trained to hunt the scent of a man through his boots and without any artificial aid such as blood."[49] Sir Charles Warren of the Metropolitan Police asked Brough to bring two of his dogs to London to test their tracking abilities. The dogs did well, but Brough and the police had a disagreement over payment for the dogs' services. Despite the dogs' success in their test, no one knows if the bloodhounds could have found Jack's scent through the crowded streets of the East End.

TAKING MORE STEPS

ONE SUGGESTION THE police received to track down Jack was to disguise policemen as prostitutes. At least one detective did go out dressed as a woman. So did one reporter who hoped to track down the killer. After the double killings, Sir Charles Warren put more officers on the street. Some wore their uniforms, others were in plain clothes. One constable recalled how he and others began nailing pieces of old bicycle tires to their shoes so they could walk without making much noise. The police also went to doss houses to interview lodgers. One former city official called for the police to search every home within a half mile of the center of Whitechapel. Such a move, though, would have been illegal, and Warren rejected it. Still, the police did search many homes, with their owners' permission

The extra police presence, however, didn't make everyone feel safe. Shop owners complained that they were losing business, and some prostitutes carried knives to protect themselves. The Mile End Vigilance Committee also put more men on the street.

Meanwhile, people kept writing to the newspapers with their thoughts about Jack's identity. Some said he might be a sailor, while the apparent skill he had in cutting the bodies made some people think he must be a doctor. There was a growing sense that he probably lived in or near Whitechapel, since he seemed to know the neighborhood so well. But he was probably not a lodger at a doss house. More likely, he lived alone or with family members who had no suspicions about his nighttime activities. Many doctors in the community agreed that Jack was insane and his madness fueled his murders.

For the month of October and into November, Jack seemed to lay low. No murders took place in Whitechapel that showed his distinctive habits. But if East Enders had any growing sense of security, Jack soon shattered it.

8

THE WORST OF ALL

Miller's Court in Spitalfields was home to several doss houses where prostitutes lived. The women entered the courtyard through a stone-paved passage that began on Dorset Street. Mary Kelly's address was 26 Dorset Street, but she used the passage to enter her room, Number 13, which looked out over Miller's Court.

The people who knew Kelly generally liked her. The twenty-four-year-old woman seemed to get along well with her neighbors, who considered her pretty, with her long ginger-colored hair, pale skin, and blue eyes. Her acquaintances also thought that Kelly was a pleasant person, though on occasion she did drink too much. And she might have had a bit of a temper, given the violent fight she had with Joseph Barnett on October 30.

Kelly and Barnett had lived together on Dorset Street for eight months before that quarrel. During that time together, Kelly told Barnett about growing up in Wales, where her family had settled after moving from Ireland when she was a child. By sixteen Kelly was married, but her husband died a few years later in a work accident. Kelly then set off for London, where she worked for a time in a brothel. In 1887 she met Barnett, and the two were soon living together. They stayed in several rooms before settling on Dorset Street.

Kelly seems to have given up prostitution until Barnett lost his job in the summer of 1888. Barnett was not happy that she wanted to earn money that way. He also disliked Kelly's letting another prostitute stay with them at Miller's Court. The woman had nowhere to live and Kelly felt sorry for her. Barnett accepted the arrangement for a few nights, but then he and Kelly argued over it.

Their fight on October 30 left a window broken, and Barnett left the room for good, though he and Kelly remained friendly.

THE NIGHT OF NOVEMBER 8

ON THE MORNING of November 8, Kelly's upstairs neighbor Elizabeth Prater paid her a visit. The day was cool and gray, and Kelly hoped that the weather would be better on Friday the ninth. That was the day of the Lord Mayor's Show. In a tradition that went back more than six hundred years, the Lord Mayor left the City of London to swear loyalty to England's king or queen. People lined the streets to watch the parade that marked the occasion.

That evening around seven thirty, Joseph Barnett stopped by his old home to see Kelly. A friend of hers named Maria Harvey was also there visiting. She left shortly after Barnett arrived. He felt bad that he didn't have any money to give Kelly, as she had fallen behind on the rent. Barnett only stayed about fifteen minutes or so. When he left, Kelly was sober, but that wouldn't last long.

Sometime after Barnett left, Kelly headed out too. By one report, she spent some time drinking in a pub on Commercial Street. Around 11:45 p.m., her neighbor Mary Ann Cox saw her back on Dorset Street. Cox, also a prostitute, was returning to her room in Miller's Court before heading out again to look for clients. Cox saw Kelly ahead of her, obviously drunk, with a man. He was short, somewhat fat, and had a moustache. He wore a long shabby coat and carried a pail filled with beer from a local pub. As Kelly and the man entered Kelly's room, Cox called out to her, "Good night, Mary Jane."[50] Kelly was so drunk she could barely say good night in return. But she could sing, as a few moments later Cox heard her start the song "A Violet from Mother's Grave."

Cox soon left her room, then came back around one a.m. Inside her room, Kelly was still singing. But sometime before two, she went back out on the streets. She knew about the Jack the Ripper murders, of course, and they scared her. But despite the late hour and any fears she had, Kelly needed more money.

When George Hutchinson spotted her near Commercial Street, Kelly was alone. She had finished her business with the man with the beer pail and was looking for another customer. Hutchinson lived in a nearby common lodging house and had often seen Kelly around the neighborhood. He had sometimes given her money, though it's not clear if he was ever one of her customers. This night Kelly asked him for a small loan, but Hutchinson had nothing to give her. "I must go and find some money," she said as she continued down the street.[51]

Hutchinson watched as a man coming from the opposite direction approached Kelly. The man tapped her on the shoulder and said something Hutchinson could not hear, and then the pair burst out laughing. Kelly and the man then headed together toward Dorset Street, passing Hutchinson. He saw that the man carried a small bag or parcel with a handle on it. The man gave Hutchinson a hard stare and pulled his hat over his face but said nothing.

Hutchinson decided to follow the couple back to Miller's Court. As they stood at the corner of the courtyard, Hutchinson heard snatches of conversation. Kelly told the man, "All right, my dear, come along, you will be comfortable."[52] The man then gave her a kiss. Kelly told him she had lost her handkerchief, and the customer gave her his. The pair went into the courtyard, and

Hutchinson again followed them, but he didn't see a light go on in Kelly's room or hear any noise. Hutchinson waited forty-five minutes to see if they would leave the room, but he gave up without seeing them again.

✦

THE NEXT MORNING

ON FRIDAY, NOVEMBER 9, John McCarthy had finally had enough. As the landlord of 26 Dorset Street, he had let Mary Kelly go three months without paying her rent. But he wanted his money, or at least some of it. In the shop he owned across the passage from Kelly's room, McCarthy ordered his assistant Thomas Bowyer to try to collect the money.

Sometime after ten a.m., Bowyer went to the door of Kelly's room and knocked. There was no answer, so he tried again. After several knocks, Bowyer went around the corner of the building and peered through a window—the one Kelly and Barnett had broken during their fight on October 30. Bowyer was stunned to see two pieces of flesh on a small table. Taking a second look, he saw blood

92

on the floor and Kelly's body on the bed. Bowyer ran to McCarthy's shop and reported what he had seen. He and McCarthy then went back across the passage so McCarthy could see for himself. The scene was as gruesome as his assistant had described. McCarthy sent Bowyer to fetch the police. At the station Detective Walter Dew waited as Bowyer tried to spit out what he had seen. Finally Bowyer said, "Another one. Jack the Ripper. Awful."[53]

Dew and Inspector Walter Beck headed to Dorset Street, calling to constables to join them along the way. At Kelly's room, Beck and Dew looked through the broken window. The scene inside the room, Dew later wrote, was "a sight which I shall never forget to my dying day."[54]

———◆———

A HORRIBLE MURDER

POLICE SURGEON GEORGE Phillips soon arrived on the scene. Since the door to Room 13 was locked, he peered through the window and saw enough to know that Kelly was dead. The police waited several hours before finally breaking down the door. Phillips and another doctor, Thomas Bond, finally had a chance to examine the body. Bond was one of the most experienced police surgeons in London, and a high-ranking police official had earlier asked him to review doctors' notes about the previous Whitechapel murders. Now Bond would have the chance to see Jack the Ripper's savage work for himself. Bond's notes from this and a later examination of Kelly's body reveal the most precise details of Jack the Ripper's bloodiest killing. (These notes had been lost until 1987, when some unknown person sent them to Scotland Yard.)

Entering the room, Bond, Phillips, and the police saw a cramped, sparsely furnished living space. Ashes from a large fire sat in the fireplace. Kelly's body was on the bed, her head turned toward the left. Blood covered the sheets and pillow, while some had splattered the walls and a pool had formed on the floor. Jack had removed the skin on Kelly's stomach and thighs and then removed the organs from her stomach. He'd also cut off her breasts, and these along with the other body parts were scattered around Kelly's body. Her face was slashed so badly that no one would have known it was her, and the deep cuts removed parts of her cheeks, eyebrows, and ears. (Joseph Barnett later identified her only by her eyes and what was left of her ears.) Along with all the other wounds, Kelly's neck had been cut down to her spine.

After completing his examination of Kelly, Dr. Bond was sure that the same person had killed her, Catherine Eddowes, Elizabeth Stride, Mary Chapman, and Mary Ann Nichols. The similarities included the slashing of the throat and the lack of a struggle. All the killings except Strides, Bond believed, were done with a similar knife, about six inches long and with a sharp point. Bond disagreed with other doctors who thought Jack the Ripper had knowledge of the human body. "In my opinion," Bond wrote, "he does not even possess the technical knowledge of a butcher or horse slaughterer or any person accustomed to cut up dead animals." But the doctor acknowledged that Jack showed "great coolness and daring" in carrying out the murders.[55]

THE EYES DON'T LIE?

The Metropolitan Police called a photographer to Mary Jane Kelly's room soon after her body was discovered. But the police didn't want to just document the crime scene. They wanted to see if a somewhat far-fetched theory might give them a clue about Jack's identity. With the development of the first cameras, some scientists wondered if a chemical in the eye could make an eye like a camera and record an image. In particular, the scientists wondered if the eye might capture the image of the last thing a person saw before his or her death. The study of this possibility was called optography, and it involved removing the eye soon after death. In the case of Mary Kelly, police seemed to hope that simply photographing her eyes might reveal the last thing she saw, which they hoped would be the face of Jack the Ripper. As Walter Dew reported, the photos did not reveal Jack's image, and copies of the pictures have never been found.

ANOTHER HUNT FOR SUSPECTS AND CLUES

IF THE BLOODY scene in Kelly's room shocked Dew and the other police, it was equally upsetting to the neighbors who saw it.

Landlord McCarthy told a newspaper that it "looked more like the work of a devil than of a man."[56] Elizabeth Prater, who had chatted with Kelly the morning of the eighth, stole a peek into the room as she went to get water from a pump in the courtyard. The little she saw made her wonder how she, a single woman who lived just above Room 13, would now be able to sleep at night.

News about the new Ripper murder soon spread through the neighborhood. People on the street watching the parade for the Lord Mayor's Show flooded Dorset Street to try to catch a glimpse of the murder scene. The crowds that gathered that day also seemed ready to take justice into their own hands. Several men who asked too many questions or otherwise seemed suspicious found large mobs gathering around them. Only the police protected the men from being beaten—or worse. As the *Daily News* reported, the crowds gather on Dorset Street thought Jack could be among them, "listening to their denunciations of him with diabolical enjoyment. This disposition of the crowd to look at each other for the criminal constituted a real peril for any stranger among them, the women specially making no secret of the longing they felt to lynch somebody."[57]

Inspector Frederick Abberline of Scotland Yard had been investigating the Whitechapel murders since the death of Mary Ann Nichols. He had begun his detective career in the East End, so he knew the area, many of the residents, and more than a few of its criminals. With this new case, one of his first steps was to see if the ashes in the fireplace held any clues. All he could find were traces of women's clothing. At the inquest on November 12, Abberline suggested that Jack had started the fire to provide light for his butchery of Kelly's body. The only other light in the room came from a small candle.

The inquest also revealed that at least two neighbors had heard a cry of "murder" around four a.m. on the morning of November 9. To Elizabeth Prater, the cry was faint, and hearing such cries, she said, was, "nothing unusual in the street. I did not take particular notice."[58] Sarah Lewis, who was visiting someone in Miller's Court, heard what was probably the same thing. She called it a shout from a young woman, but like Prater she didn't think much of it. Lewis also reported seeing a man with a black bag in the neighborhood the previous Wednesday, then saw him again the night of Kelly's murder. Could that have been the man with a bag that George Hutchinson saw approach Kelly on the street?

The timing of Kelly's death was hard to pin down. Dr. Bond thought it could have been as early as one a.m., though that would contradict Hutchinson's statement of seeing Kelly with a man after two a.m. The earlier time also conflicted with the time of the "murder" cry that two people heard, though there was no evidence that Kelly had uttered it. Finally, another statement at the inquest confused the issue. Caroline Maxwell of Dorset Street knew Kelly and said she saw her on the street around eight thirty on the morning of the ninth—only two hours or so before Thomas Bowyer found her body.

As with the past murders, all the statements from the witnesses added up to nothing concrete. The day before Kelly's murder, Sir Charles Warren had resigned as police commissioner, in part because of his efforts to defend the Metropolitan Police's handling of the case. His own defenders, such as the *Spectator*, said he had "done all that man can do to protect Whitechapel."[59] Warren's resignation did not take effect until later in November. One of his last acts regarding the Ripper the case was to issue a public statement on the tenth. The government would not jail anyone who helped Jack commit his crimes, if the **accomplice** provided evidence that led to Jack's conviction.

Meanwhile, the latest Ripper murder led to more international attention on the Whitechapel killings. Newspapers across the United States and Canada carried the news, as did some in Europe. The *New York World* of November 11 noted Warren's sense of "utter hopelessness" in solving the crimes. The paper also wrote, "[Jack's] latest escapade . . . proves that he is a shrewd man, and not above changing his tactics. Knowing that the streets are closely watched, he lures his victims to their rooms." The paper added, making a prediction that turned out to be true: "He will probably not be caught unless by some blunder of his own."[60] Jack, the world learned, did not make a blunder.

9

IS JACK STILL AT WORK?

The mystery of Jack the Ripper's identity was still unsolved as the new year of 1889 began. In the days and weeks after the Mary Jane Kelly mutilation, concerned citizens continued to bombard the police with letters offering tips and suggestions. The police questioned men in the East End who acted suspiciously around women or who seemed to fit some of the descriptions of men seen with the victims. As fall turned into winter, the police kept up their patrols of the streets of Whitechapel, but their numbers shrank over tine. The officers who remained on the street discovered nothing.

Murders still took place in the neighborhood, but none of them seemed to fit the pattern of Jack's crimes. One that caught the public's attention anyway involved the discovery over several weeks of various female body parts in the Thames River. A few US newspapers quickly blamed Jack for the crime, and reports circulated that the police had received a letter signed "Jack the Ripper" before the first body parts were discovered. The letter said that Jack was not dead, implying he would strike again. The police, though, did not take this and a second letter from the same writer seriously, and the newspaper's attention soon turned to another possible new Ripper victim.

WAS IT JACK?

IN JULY OF 1889 one case seemed closer to Jack's usual mode of killing than any other since the Kelly murder: the death of Alice McKenzie.

Like the previous Ripper victims, McKenzie lived in an East End doss house and earned at least some of her money as a prostitute. She also had a fondness for smoking pipes, which led to her nickname of Claypipe Alice. On July 16, after a quarrel with her live-in boyfriend, Alice went out drinking. Several people saw her during the afternoon and into the evening, with the last known sighting of her coming just before midnight. At the time, McKenzie was alone and in a hurry. The next time anyone saw her, about an hour later, she was dead, her body lying on the street in Castle Alley.

McKenzie had a slash across her neck and a horizontal cut down the front of her torso. The cut to the neck, however, was not as deep as the ones on Jack's other victims. The cut in the abdomen was also nothing like the savage rippings Jack had inflicted on his victims. Police surgeon George Phillips, who had examined some of those women, thought that this killer had some knowledge of the body, since he had cut McKenzie's throat in a way that killed her quickly. But he thought the murder weapon was most likely a smaller knife than the one used in the past. After his examination, Phillips declared, "I cannot satisfy myself . . . that the perpetrator of all the 'Wh Ch. [Whitechapel] murders' is our man. I am on the contrary impelled to a contrary conclusion ..."[61]

Dr. Thomas Bond, however, who had become actively involved with the Whitechapel murders during the Kelly case, had a different conclusion. He told police officials, "I am of opinion that the murder was performed by the same person who committed the former series of Whitechapel murder[s]."[62] The disagreement over whether Jack had struck again split high-ranking police officials as well, with some supporting Phillips and others Bond. James Monro, who oversaw plain-clothes detectives on the Metropolitan force, was one who thought Jack had returned. Monro once again ordered increased patrols in Whitechapel.

When no other Ripper-like murders took place, Monro once again cut back the patrols. The East End seemed to be free of Jack all through 1890, but then in February of 1891 another prostitute turned up dead in a way that reminded many of Jack.

Frances Coles was born and raised in London and at one time she'd worked packaging medicines for sale. Some time in her early twenties, however, she became a prostitute in

Whitechapel—something she hid from her family. But on a visit to her sister on December 26, 1890, Mary Ann Coles must have sensed something was wrong in Frances's life. Mary Ann later reported that her sister seemed poor and was very dirty. Frances Coles also drank, so much so that at times others near her smelled the alcohol on her.

Starting on February 11, Coles shared more than a few drinks with James Sadler, a sailor on a cargo ship and a former customer. The pair spent that night and much of the next day together. After a fight, however, the two split up. Coles spent the rest of the twelfth either drunk or passed out from her drinking. Finally, early on the morning of the thirteenth, she left the common lodging house where she was staying to get some food.

At 2:15 Constable Ernest Thompson was patrolling west of Commercial Street on Chamber Street. He heard footsteps but could not see anyone. Then he turned into an area known as Swallow Gardens, a passage that ran beneath elevated railway tracks. There Thompson saw a body. As he got closer and shone his lamp, he could see that it was a woman. She opened and then closed one eye. Thompson could also see blood by the body, and he blew his whistle for help. Frances Cole, though, died before help could arrive.

The next day, at least one newspaper was quick to say, "Jack the Ripper Again."[63] But Dr. Phillips did not see any clear parallels with Jack's other victims, other than cuts to Coles's throat.

People who knew Coles soon stepped forward and reported that she had been with Sadler before the murder. The police arrested him, and for a time wondered if he could have been Jack. Jack or not, area women came down to the police station and demanded that Sadler be hung for the murder. In the end though, the police couldn't produce enough solid evidence to link Sadler to Coles's death. As far as his being Jack, records showed that Sadler had been out at sea when four of the Whitechapel murders occurred.

As for Constable Thompson, who found Coles's body, some people later suggested that he regretted not trying to find the person who made the footsteps he heard. Could it have been Jack? But why should he have been suspicious before he knew a crime had been committed? Whoever the person was, he was not running as if he were fleeing a murder scene. Still, a San

Francisco newspaper reported on February 14 that Thompson was "the most unhappy man in London tonight, as he feels he had the most noted criminal of the age within his grasp."[64]

⸺◆⸺

A DEAD END

AFTER THE COLES case, no other murders in the East End that year seemed close to Jack's work. While the police kept the case open, Jack the Ripper seemed to have stopped his murderous ways. Had he left London? Was he imprisoned for some other crime? Was he dead? No one knew. Was the killer even the same person in all five of the Whitechapel murders thought to be committed by Jack? Dr. Phillips, after his work on the various cases, thought there could have been more than one killer, though that theory is not widely held today. And police officials then still disagreed as to which Whitechapel murders should be linked to Jack. In 1892, Chief Inspector Frederick Abberline said the McKenzie and Coles killings were not committed by Jack, and some officials thought either Mary Ann Nichols or Mary Jane

Kelly were not Jack's victims, bringing his death toll to just four.

To Ripperologist Philip Sugden, there's also the chance that Jack started his crimes with attacks that didn't lead to deaths. In the spring of 1888, two women from Whitechapel were assaulted by a man wielding a knife. In both cases the attacker was a stranger to the victim. Could Jack have started his frenzy with these attacks, then gotten more violent with his killing until the final mutilation of Kelly? Sugden says it's possible. Melville Macnaghten, who joined the City of London police force after Jack's killings, wrote a report on the killings in 1894. He noted the progression in Jack's butchery and said Jack's "appetite" for the murders was only sharpened with each crime. Given that, Macnaghten suggested that the killings stopped for only one reason: "The murderer's brain gave way altogether after his awful glut in Miller's Court, and that he immediately committed suicide, or, as a possible alternative, was found to be so hopelessly mad by his relations that he was by them confined in some asylum."[65]

During and after the five murders usually linked to Jack, the various London police departments involved faced criticism for not finding a likely suspect. But in a newspaper report of

November 4, 1888, just before the Kelly murder, the *Pall Mall Gazette* described a tour Chief Inspector Henry Moore of Scotland Yard gave to American journalist R. Harding Davis. Moore wanted Davis to see the challenges of working in the crowded and sometimes dark streets of Whitechapel.

The British newspaper reported that "Moore led the journalist through the network of narrow passageways as dark and loathsome as the great network of sewers that stretches underneath them a few feet below." Moore recounted how a police officer from Texas who saw those narrow alleys said, "'I never saw anything like it before. We've nothing like it in all America.' He said that at home an officer could stand on a street corner and look down four different streets and see all that went on in them for a quarter of a mile off."[66] That kind of observation was impossible in parts of Whitechapel.

Moore said that after one murder, his men thought they had blocked off every entrance to the crime scene, but soon dozens of people had found their way through the police lines, using passages the police never discovered. If Jack lived in the neighborhoods where he committed his crimes, as some officers thought, then he would probably find it easy to elude the police on the streets. Moore also pointed out that many people in the neighborhood didn't lock their doors at night. He said, "The murderer has only to lift the latch of the nearest house and walk through it and out the back way."[67]

THE LONDON FOG

Books and films set in Victorian London often feature foggy nights, which create an atmosphere of mystery and perhaps even horror. That image of fog has often been associated with Jack the Ripper and his crimes. The thick fog that was common during that era was more a creation of human activities than the weather, as people often burned coal for heat and used it to fuel factory machines and steam-powered vehicles. Today this fog would more commonly be called smog—a combination of fog and air pollution. At its worst, the London fog caused accidents on the streets and added to health problems. The fog often had a yellow color, caused by the chemical sulfur in the air. So did the famous London fogs help hide the identity of Jack the Ripper? It's doubtful. While his crimes sometimes took place on rainy nights and mornings, there's no evidence that thick fogs appeared during those times. The worst fogs of the era came during the winter, though an article in the *Daily Telegraph* noted a sudden, thick fog descended on London's West End and the City of London on November 1, 1888, forcing people to use gas lights and lamps during the daytime.

Moore explained to the visiting journalist that the women on the street made Jack's work even easier for him. The women, he said, "lead him, of their own free will, to the spot where they know interruption is least likely. It is not as if he had to wait for his chance; they make the chance for him. And then they are so miserable and so hopeless, so utterly lost to all that makes a person want to live, that . . . [they] will go in any man's company, and run the risk that it is not him." When Moore met prostitutes on the street, he told them to go home, but many did not have a home. Being so desperate for money, they risked choosing Jack as a customer. When Davis asked Moore about clues, items Jack might have left behind, the detective admitted they had none: "He never leaves so much as a rag behind him. There is no more of a clue to that chap's identity than there is to the identity of some murderer who will kill someone a hundred years from now."[68]

Moore continued, "And then we are so often misled by false clues, suggested by people who have a spite to work off. We get any number of letters throwing the most circumstantial evidence about a certain man, and when we run it out we find some woman whom he has thrown over. All this takes time and money, and from the nature of our work we can say nothing of what we are doing; we can only speak when it is done. I have received two thousand letters of advice from America alone; you can fancy how many I get from this country."[69] Stressing the confusion created by false leads, random advice, and so many people involved, Inspector Abberline said, ". . . we were almost lost in theories: There were so many of them." [70]

10

THE FIRST NAMED
SUSPECTS

Despite never making an arrest at the time of the Whitechapel murders, some police officials privately considered several suspects. In 1894, Sir Melville Macnaghten was the chief constable for Metropolitan Police's Criminal Investigation Division (CID). Although he did not investigate the Ripper murders as they occurred, he had access to private police records. He wrote a report to answer a newspaper's claim that it knew Jack's identity. The *Sun* suggested that Thomas Cutbush was the murderer, though it didn't use his name. Macnaghten's naming of other suspects in response has become a starting point for people trying to pinpoint Jack's identity.

———◆———

WHO WAS CUTBUSH?

THE *SUN* NEWSPAPER began publishing a series of articles in February of 1894 that sought to challenge "the general impression for a long time . . . that Jack the Ripper is dead." Instead, the paper argued that Jack most likely had been locked up for several years. According to the *Sun*, it had found Jack in an insane asylum, and while the paper did not give his real identity, it said several of its reporters spoke with Jack there. One article said, "We gazed through the iron bars at the slowly moving figure beneath the opposite wall. The ghosts of the victims of this wretched man seemed to troop by his side in the gloom and solitude."[71]

In their writings about Jack the Ripper, both the police and newspapers sometimes referred to him or anyone who could commit such crimes as mad or insane, and called him a maniac or a lunatic. Those terms are not used today; doctors talk about mental illness, not madness or lunacy. While Victorian doctors knew that mental illness existed, they did not always have names for the specific illnesses that people developed, or know their causes. They certainly didn't have the medicines available now, and the use of "talk therapy"—talking about mental and emotional problems as a way to treat some issues—was just beginning in Jack's time. If patients were considered incurable, they might receive no treatment at all and stay in an asylum—or "madhouse"—until they died. The goal with the most severe cases was to keep them under control, which sometimes meant putting them in solitary confinement. People with money could go to small private asylums and receive better attention. The poor and those labeled criminally insane went to much larger publicly run facilities. Today hospitalization is only used for the most severe patients, and the goal is to find a treatment that will help them return to their normal activities.

With the details the *Sun* provided, people realized that the paper was suggesting that Thomas Cutbush was Jack. In March of 1891 Cutbush was sent to Lambeth Infirmary in London. He was held as a lunatic but soon managed to escape. While on the loose, he stabbed one women in the buttocks and attempted to stab another. Cutbush seemed to be copying the crimes of a man who had recently been arrested for carrying out similar stabbings.

Cutbush was caught, found insane by the courts, and sent to Broadmoor Criminal Lunatic Asylum—the same place where the *Sun* met the supposed Jack the Ripper. Cutbush had a history of mental illness dating back to 1888, thinking people were trying to poison him. He enjoyed reading medical books and often walked the streets at night, but he was much younger than the suspects seen with Jack's victims right before their murders. Police had no reason to link Cutbush to Jack's crimes. Yet the *Sun*'s stories seemed to upset some members of the Metropolitan Police—perhaps because Cutbush was the nephew of one of their former top officials.

<hr />

THE MACNAGHTEN MEMO

IN RESPONSE TO the *Sun*'s articles, Macnaghten wrote a memo for police use explaining why Cutbush was not Jack. He also gave the names of three men that the Metropolitan Police had considered much more likely suspects—though not necessarily the only suspects. While police officials knew these names, they did not become public until decades later. Macnaghten wrote two different sets of notes describing the suspects. One was placed in official police records, while the other he kept. Those notes stayed in his family after his death and were later shared with two writers. In 1965, American author Tom Cullen was the first person to print the names of the three men Macnaghten named as suspects. They were M. J. Druitt, a man identified only as Kosminski, and Michael Ostrog. Macnaghten gave only a brief description of the three men, but historians and Ripperologists have tracked down more information about them. The experts have also offered what they consider proof that each one was—or was not—Jack the Ripper.

———✦———

THE DEPRESSED BARRISTER

MACNAGHTEN DESCRIBED MONTAGUE John Druitt as "sexually insane" and noted that he committed suicide shortly after the November 1888 murder of Mary Jane Kelly. He added, "From private information, I have little doubt but that his own family believed him to have been the murderer."[72] Not all of the inspector's information was accurate, as he called Druitt a doctor, but he was the son of a doctor, and a cousin with the same last named practiced medicine in London until 1886. Druitt was actually a barrister, a lawyer in England who can represent clients in court. He also worked as a headmaster at a private school that helped boys with bad grades prepare for exams. He was suddenly fired from his job at the school in November 1888 for some unknown "serious trouble," which may have spurred the depression that led to his suicide.[73] He may also have been upset about his mother, who had been sent to an insane asylum that summer. In a suicide note found at his apartment and addressed to his brother William, Druitt wrote: "Since Friday I felt I was going to be like mother, and the best thing for me was to die."[74] Suicide and mental illness seemed to run in the family, and perhaps Druitt felt the strain of that during a difficult time in his life.

Druitt was last seen alive on December 3. On the last day of the year, around one p.m., a man who worked along the Thames River pulled out Druitt's decomposing body. Nothing on his body or in his apartment suggested that he had any ties to the Whitechapel murders. Still, the fact that Macnaghten listed him as the first suspect later raised eyebrows. So did a comment Macnaghten made years later, when he said he was sorry he had joined the CID after the suicide of Jack the Ripper, so he'd never had a chance to track him down. The mention of suicide seemed to refer back to Druitt, and Macnaghten mentioned Jack's suicide to the press in 1913. He added, "I have destroyed all my documents, and there is now no record of the secret information which came into my possession at one time or another."[75]

Whatever this secret information was, no police evidence exists to confirm that Druitt was Jack. And his playing at several cricket matches outside of London on or after the date of several of the killings suggests to modern-day doubters that Druitt was not the killer. He would not have had time to clean up from his murders and get to the matches. In 1903, Inspector Frederick Abberline commented on the notion that Druitt or any other dead suspect was Jack: "It is simple nonsense to talk of the police having proof that the man is dead. I am, and always have been, in the closest touch with Scotland Yard, and it would have been next to impossible for me not to have known all about it. Besides, the authorities would have been only too glad to make an end of such a mystery, if only for their own credit."[76]

<hr>

THE DELUSIONAL HAIRDRESSER

MOVING ON TO the second suspect, Macnaghten referred to Kosminski as "a Polish Jew—and resident in Whitechapel."

Kosminski, the inspector continued, had a great hatred of women and was insane. "There were many circumstances connected with this man which made him a strong 'suspect,'" Macnaghten wrote. Kosminski ended up in an asylum.

Almost twenty years later, in 1910, Sir Robert Anderson shared his views on the killer's identity. Anderson was one of the top officials at the CID when Jack committed his murders, and he wrote a book about his own life. He said that the police had identified Jack as a Polish Jew from Whitechapel, though he did not give a name. While Kosminski was in the asylum, Anderson wrote, "the only person who ever had a good view of the murderer unhesitatingly identified the suspect the instant he was confronted with him; but he refused to give evidence against him."[77]

If he knew Jack's identity, and if the Polish Jew he was referring to was Kosminski, why didn't Anderson say so? He wrote that doing so would serve no public benefit, "and the traditions of my old department would suffer."[78] Another man who seemed to know whom Anderson meant was Chief Inspector Donald Swanson. He owned a copy of Anderson's book and made notes on the pages. The book ended up with Swanson's grandson, who in 1987 shared the notes with a London paper.

Swanson's written comments indicate that the man who identified the suspect in the asylum was also Jewish. He did not want to provide evidence that would send another Jew to his death for the Whitechapel murders. But Swanson leaves no doubt who the suspect was, as he names him: Kosminski.

Since then, Ripperologists have used these few clues to try to pin down the identity of this Kosminski and determine if he really was Jack. Adding to the problem is that some students of Jack the Ripper believe he may actually have been a Jewish Whitechapel resident named Nathan Kaminsky, who entered an insane asylum in December 1888 and died there about a year later. Macnaghten said that the "Polish Jew" he meant was committed in 1889, which is why there is some suspicion that he meant Kaminsky, since he was admitted to an asylum closer to that date. The only likely Kosminski was not committed until 1891.

If a man named Kosminski was the suspect, most experts believe he was a hairdresser named Aaron Kosminski. Records show that he entered a workhouse in 1890 and was considered insane. The next year he was sent to Colney Hatch, an insane asylum. Kosminski's mental illness would probably lead modern doctors to call him schizophrenic. He believed some outside force controlled his actions and that voices told him not to eat food that others prepared for him. Because of that, Kosminski scrounged for scraps of food in the streets. His mental state kept him from working, and he was often dirty.

While the date Kosminski went to the asylum does not match the one Macnaghten gave, Colney Hatch is the asylum Swanson mentioned in his notes. But Nathan Kaminsky had been there too. Kosminski also did not show violent tendencies and was actually released in 1894, though he went to another facility for the mentally ill. That fact conflicts with Swanson's claim that the Kosminski he named died at Colney Hatch.

<hr>

WAS JACK AARON KOSMINSKI?

DESPITE THE KOSMINSKI/KAMINSKY confusion, by the 1990s a number of Ripperologists thought Aaron Kosminski was the most likely suspect. Some, though, were not convinced that Aaron was the right Kosminski, pointing out that the depth of his mental illness made it unlikely he could successfully carry out the murders without leaving a clue. Others noted that not all police statements regarding him and other details about the case were accurate. This seemed to be particularly true of Sir Robert Anderson, who wrote about Jack many years after the killing.

In 2014, however, an English businessman named Russell Edwards claimed to have proof that Aaron Kosminski was Jack the Ripper. Modern science, in the form of DNA testing, had provided the answer. DNA is a string of molecules that forms genes. Genes control the production of proteins that determine how cells function. Genes and DNA determine what traits a person has, such as their height or the color of their hair. Parents pass on copies of their genes to their children, and relatives share similar DNA. Edwards convinced living relatives of Kosminski to provide samples of their DNA to see if it matched DNA found on a shawl that supposedly belonged to Ripper victim Catherine Eddowes.

The story of the shawl goes back to a police constable named Amos Simpson who said he was on special duty the night of the Eddowes murder. According to his family, Simpson came upon Eddowes's dead body in Mitre Square and took home the shawl as a souvenir. The blood-stained cloth was passed on through the family for more than a hundred years, never being washed, until the last owner put it up for sale in 2007. Edwards bought it, then called in biologist Dr. Jari Louhelainen to do DNA detective work. Could he verify that stains on the shawl contained traces of DNA that came from both Eddowes and Kosminski? In his book *Naming the Ripper*, Edwards said that the scientist did. Edwards said that the DNA proved Kosminski was the killer.

Few people, though, accepted the evidence he presented. The unwashed shawl could have picked up bits of DNA from many people over the years. And the kind of DNA Louhelainen worked with does not provide absolute proof of people being related. His findings would not be accepted in a court of law, and most Ripperologists rejected them as well. Several scientists familiar with DNA analysis also found that Louhelainen made a mistake in his calculations when comparing the DNA on the shawl with a sample taken from one of Eddowes's living relatives. In other words, there was not even proof that the shawl had belonged to Jack's victim, despite the beliefs of Constable Simpson's family. The question of whether Jack was Aaron Kosminski was still unsolved.

———◆———

THE "RUSSIAN DOCTOR"

THE LAST SUSPECT Macnaghten named in 1894 was Michael Ostrog. He called Ostrog "a Russian doctor, and a convict, who was subsequently detained in a lunatic asylum as a **homicidal maniac.**" Police records show that Ostrog did have a long history of breaking the law, though most of his arrests were for stealing jewelry and other small items. During his life of crime, he used many false names and told tall tales to convince people to give him money. He was smart and charming, traits that helped him in his criminal activities. He also seemed to fake mental illness at times if he thought it would mean a shorter prison sentence.

An article in the *Police Gazette* in October 1888, at the height of the Jack the Ripper panic, noted that Ostrog was wanted by the police for failing to report to them as he was supposed to. He had been released earlier in the year from an insane asylum, where he had been sent after another petty theft. Ripperologist Philip Sugden suggested that the police were looking for Ostrog in October because they wanted to question him as a suspect in the Ripper murders. Ostrog apparently passed himself off as a doctor at times, and the police thought that Jack might have had medical skills. Ostrog, having recently left the asylum, also fit the police profile that Jack was probably insane.

There is no proof, however, that Ostrog actually had any medical skills or that he really was insane when he was committed in the fall of 1887. There is also no proof that Ostrog was a homicidal maniac, as Macnaghten claimed. Ostrog was also almost six feet tall—well above average for a man of that era, and much taller than the height witnesses gave for the suspects they saw. The final proof that Michael Ostrog was not Jack the Ripper came long after Macnaghten wrote his memo. Researchers found that Ostrog, again using a false name, was in a French jail during the time of the Ripper murders.

Despite the belief of some people that either M. J. Druitt or someone named Kosminski could have been Jack, no one has provided solid proof. That left the door open for police officers and amateur detectives to present a long list of possible suspects.

11

NEW SUSPECTS EMERGE

Almost ten years passed between Sir Melville Macnaghten writing his memo and the public hearing about another man some thought could be Jack the Ripper. His name was George Chapman, and Jack or not, he was responsible for his own horrible crimes.

Chapman was trained as a barber, but in 1902 he ran the Monumental Tavern in London. Helping out was a woman he called his wife, Maud Marsh. They lived together as if they were married, though Chapman had never divorced his actual wife, whom he had married thirteen years before.

That fall Marsh became ill. Chapman called on Dr. James Stoker, who couldn't pin down her illness, but a second doctor called in by Marsh's family thought something was suspicious. Dr. Francis Grapel thought Marsh showed signs of being poisoned. He expressed his concerns to Stoker. When Marsh died suddenly the next day, Stoker wanted a careful medical analysis of her body. Experts found signs of poison in several organs, and Chapman became the police's prime suspect.

Soon the suspicions about Chapman grew. Twice before, he had lived with young women and had pretended to be married to them. Each time, his "wife" died after a mysterious illness. The police ordered the dead bodies of these two women to be **exhumed** and examined. In one case the woman had been dead five years, yet her corpse had barely rotted in the ground. She and the other woman had been poisoned with the same chemical that killed Maud Marsh. The poison, called antimony, had preserved their bodies.

George Chapman went on trial in March 1903, was found

guilty of murder, and was executed in April. His carefully planned killing of three women was horrible enough, but then Detective Frederick Abberline stirred more interest in Chapman when he said that Chapman could be Jack the Ripper.

<hr />

WAS CHAPMAN JACK?

ABBERLINE GAVE AN interview to the *Pall Mall Gazette* that was published on March 24, 1903. He said that since he first heard about the details of Chapman's life, "the idea has taken full possession of me, and everything fits in and dovetails so well that I cannot help feeling that this is the man we struggled so hard to capture fifteen years ago."[79] Abberline noted that the Ripper murders began soon after Chapman arrived in London from Poland and ended when he briefly moved to America. Chapman had also trained as a surgeon, and several times the doctors who examined Jack's victims suggested he might have medical knowledge and skill with a surgeon's knife.

While Abberline did not have solid proof that Jack and

Chapman were the same person, he thought that the facts he mentioned suggested Chapman could not be ruled out. In a second interview with the paper he said, "A man who could watch his wives being slowly tortured to death by poison, as he did, was capable of anything."[80] Abberline also pointed out that Chapman had threatened to attack his actual wife with a knife when they were living in America. To Abberline, if Chapman were Jack, he simply swapped his knife for poison. His "fiendishness" still existed, Abberline believed. And "the victims, too, you will notice, continue to be women; but they are of different classes, and obviously call for different methods of despatch [murder]."

What else was known about George Chapman? For one, his real name was Severin Klosowski. He trained as a surgeon in Poland but worked as a barber in London after he moved there in 1887 or early 1888. He lived and worked in the East End before he and his wife, Lucy, went to America in 1891, settling in New Jersey. Lucy returned without him in 1892—after Chapman's threatened knife attack. Chapman later returned too, and the couple briefly lived together again. They soon broke up for good without getting a divorce. In 1893, Chapman met Annie

Chapman—no relation to the Ripper victim of the same name. After that relationship ended, Severin Klosowski borrowed her last name and became George Chapman.

Chapman began his poisonings at the end of 1897 with Mary Spink, followed just over four years later with Bessie Taylor. At Chapman's trial in 1903, witnesses testified that he sometimes acted violently toward all of his pretend wives. With this history of violence and murder, some people thought back to the unsolved Jack the Ripper killings and wondered if Chapman had been Jack.

Even before Abberline shared his thoughts, other police detectives made the link. A story on March 23, 1903, in the *Daily Chronicle* went into detail about Chapman's threatening his wife, Lucy, with a knife. The story said that "the police have considerable doubt whether the full extent of the criminality of Klosowski has been nearly revealed by the recent investigations . . ."[81] The police learned from Lucy Klosowski that during the time of the Whitechapel murders, her husband stayed out until the early morning without giving a reason. And at least one witness remembered him carrying a black bag. A witness to the Ripper murders also said that a suspect in the Mary Kelly killing carried a black bag.

Abberline and others have noted that the Whitechapel murders stopped after Chapman went to America. That could suggest a tie between Jack and Chapman. Trying to strengthen the connection, some people have asserted that Ripper-like murders started in the New York area while Chapman was there. There is evidence of one killing of a New York prostitute that, to local papers, called to mind Jack the Ripper. But nothing links Chapman to that and it was not followed by similar killings.

Whatever similarities between Jack and George Chapman, no one has ever produced solid evidence to link Chapman to Jack's crimes. Other problems come from details witnesses gave about Jack that don't match Chapman—or vice versa. At the time of the murders, Chapman was 23—younger than how most witnesses describe Jack. And Lucy Klosowski's comments about her husband's late-night activities are questionable, as they seem to have met for the first time after the last of the Ripper murders.

Even with the doubts, some Ripperologists say Chapman is a likely candidate to have been Jack the Ripper. But in the end, no one can say he was Jack. And confusing the story about Chapman as Jack are the claims made in a 1959 book, *Identity of Jack the Ripper* by Donald McCormick.

The author cited unpublished notes from Dr. Thomas Dutton, who said he had seen some of the letters supposedly written by Jack the Ripper. Dutton also claimed to be a friend of Frederick Abberline and said the detective later abandoned the theory that Chapman was Jack. Instead, he thought Chapman had a double, a man who was also a surgeon and came from Russia (part of Poland was controlled by Russia when Chapman/Klosowski was born). Perhaps, Dutton wondered, the double was Michael Ostrog, the doctor mentioned in the Macnaghten memo. Or it could be a certain Alexander Pedachenko, a Russian spy sent to London around the time of the murders. That suggestion had first been made during the 1920s, and Dutton knew about it.

According to the "double" theory, which Dutton supposedly believed, the double sometimes pretended to be Chapman, and he could have carried out the Ripper murders. In his book, McCormick shoots down the theory, but he presents other facts that Ripperologists now say are false. Donald Rumbelow said the book "is almost worthless as a research tool."[82] Another Ripperologist, Melvin Harris, said McCormick presents "a series of lies."[83]

McCormick's book shows one of the problems with trying to learn the identity of Jack the Ripper. Many people are just out to sell books, not find the truth. Claiming to have a new theory or proof about Jack's identity is sure to draw attention. That desire to present theories about who really carried out the Whitechapel murders has led to bizarre notions and sometimes fakery.

A "CONFESSION" BEFORE DYING?

Also on the long list of possible, if highly unlikely, suspects is Dr. Neill Cream. Like George Chapman, Cream was a convicted murderer. Born in Scotland, he grew up in Canada and later moved to the United States. He was convicted of poisoning a woman there and then of killing four British prostitutes the same way after he came to London in 1891. In November of 1892, as he was about to be hanged, Cream supposedly said "I am Jack . . ." and then the noose tightened around his neck, killing him. Was Cream about to confess to being Jack the Ripper? Some people have thought so—despite the fact that he was in an Illinois prison in 1888, when Jack carried out his bloody killing spree. For some people, though, facts don't get in the way of a good story. So they have suggested that, like Chapman, Cream had a double, and that the double carried out the murders. Since he was going to die anyway, Cream was about to confess to the killings to remove any suspicion from the double. Another suggestion was that Cream was able to bribe prison officials, escape his Illinois cell, and then make his way to London before the end of his sentence. With his illegally gained freedom, Cream then would have been able to carry out the Whitechapel murders. Once again, no one has any proof for this theory.

WAS JACK A JILL?

MCCORMICK'S BOOK ALSO brought up an idea that people had first discussed while the murders were still going on: Could the murderer be a woman? In a letter to the *Evening News* published on October 16, 1888, a reader suggested the killer could be a woman: "The idea is not to be laughed at. A woman accustomed to midwifery I think is more capable and likely to inflict the dreadful mutilation which has attended these murders (when thirsting for blood) than a man. . . . The woman may have influence over her fellow sex, or might easily have by mixing amongst them as 'pals.'"[84] McCormick wrote that Frederick Abberline and Dr. Dutton discussed a similar notion. The detective referred to the testimony of a witness in the Mary Kelly murder, Caroline Maxwell. She was a neighbor of Kelly's and she claimed that she saw Kelly, or a woman who looked like her, on the streets hours after Jack supposedly killed her. Maxwell said she was sure that she had previously seen Kelly wearing the shawl she saw on the woman that morning.

Abberline, according to McCormick, wondered if the killer was a woman and had put on Kelly's clothes to try to escape undetected. Dutton thought that was not likely, but that if Jack the Ripper were actually "Jill the Ripper," she was most probably a midwife. Then as now, midwives were trained to help pregnant women deliver their babies. Some midwives also performed abortions, which were illegal at the time. A midwife in Victorian times could be on the streets at any hour to help deliver babies. They might also have blood on the their clothes after a delivery. Because of those facts, they would not arouse suspicion. Could Mary Kelly have been pregnant and wanted an abortion? That's the theory of William Stewart, who discussed the chance that Jack was a woman two decades before McCormick wrote his book. The midwife, Stewart said, killed Kelly and then left her room wearing some of Kelly's clothes. She had probably killed some of the other Whitechapel victims too. Stewart even suggests a possible "Jill": a midwife named Mary Pearcey, who was executed for murder in 1890, though not for a Whitechapel victim.

In 1972, a former London detective named Arthur Butler laid out his theory for a female murderer. He said that two of the five Ripper victims died because of an abortion that went wrong. To cover up her unskillful work, the midwife killed her patients. This unknown killer then murdered two of the other victims because they knew what happened.

As with many theories connected to the Whitechapel murders, the idea of a Jill the Ripper has several problems. The first four Ripper victims were not pregnant. And there is no proof that Kelly was, though rumors of it are still mentioned by some amateur Ripperologists. Beyond that, there is no evidence of botched abortions or sightings of women with the victims close to the times of the murders.

———◆———

THE ROYAL SUSPECT

MCCORMICK'S BOOK WAS hardly the last source that presented supposed evidence about Jack's identity. In 1970, Dr. Thomas Stowell wrote an article that did not name a suspect, but the details he gave led some to believe that he meant a man some knew as Eddy. The claim created a stir because Eddy was better known as Prince Albert Victor Christian Edward, Duke of Clarence, the grandson of Queen Victoria! Just before he died, Stowell said that he was not referring to the prince, but that did not stop people from thinking he was. Stowell said that his information came from notes left behind by Sir William Gull, who had served as Queen Victoria's doctor. Stowell had also apparently told others about the idea that the prince could be Jack several years before he wrote his article.

Even before that article appeared, a French writer named Phillip Jullian wrote that rumors had circulated in London that Prince Eddy was the murderer. And in Stowell's account, the Royal Family knew Eddy was the killer after the second slaying. After the night of the double killings, the family had the prince locked away in a private asylum. Stowell claimed that Eddy's madness came from syphilis, a disease that can affect the brain, but there is no proof he had the disease.

Once again, known facts seem to contradict the theory. The prince was on a hunting trip in Scotland and in the English countryside on the dates of several of the murders. And if the prince was showing signs of madness and his family knew he was a homicidal maniac, would the prince's father have sent him to Denmark as his representative?

If the facts seem to rule out Eddy's role in the murders, perhaps people close to him were responsible. Some people have claimed that Stowell's unnamed suspect, whom he called "S," was the prince's good friend, James Kenneth Stephen. A brain injury led to a mental illness that eventually forced Stephen into an asylum. Others say that the queen's doctor, Sir William Gull, could have been the killer. His role was supposedly part of a larger plot to keep Prince Eddy out of trouble.

According to this story, the prince had a secret marriage to a common woman named Annie Crook. Along with not being royalty, Crook was a Roman Catholic. By law, a potential heir to the British throne cannot marry a Catholic, unless he or she gives up their claim to the throne. So Gull, an artist named Walter Sickert, and a coachman named John Netley tried to cover up the marriage and the baby that the prince and Crook supposedly had. (Crook did indeed have a baby, in 1885, and the father's name is not listed on the birth certificate.) Government officials stepped in, and Gull performed a surgery on Crook's brain to destroy her memory.

The supposed tie to the Whitechapel murders comes with the last victim, Mary Kelly. She was said to be Crook's nursemaid, who took care of her young daughter. Since Kelly knew about the marriage, Gull and the others wanted to kill her. The four other victims were targeted because Kelly recruited them to help her blackmail the royal family. In return for money, the women would not reveal what they knew about Prince Eddy's wife and baby. To prevent any information about the prince getting out, Gull, with Sickert and Netley's help, tracked down the women and killed them.

This elaborate scheme was outlined in a Stephen Knight's 1976 book, *Jack the Ripper: The Final Solution*. Since then, Ripperologists have noted that while Knight listed certain facts that could be verified—such as the existence of Annie Crook and her daughter—most of the story is based on assumptions. As far as other documents and proof, Knight claims that the plot's organizers destroyed any evidence that would reveal details of the plot. This explanation of the Ripper murders has the features of a typical conspiracy theory: The plotters get rid of information and evidence that might reveal the nature of the conspiracy. Respected Ripperologist Philip Sugden noted that Knight himself found evidence that showed his story was false. But he wrote the book anyway, spreading "falsehoods and absurdities" that people can still read today.[85]

THE AMERICAN RIPPER

A LETTER DISCOVERED in 1993 pointed suspicion toward a new Ripper suspect. George Sims was a journalist at the time of the Whitechapel murders. He often wrote about social conditions in London during the Victoria era, and he reported on Jack the Ripper. Sims even found himself a suspect for a brief moment, when a merchant saw a drawing of Sims promoting one of his books and thought it looked like someone the merchant suspected of being the killer. Sims wrote about the incident years later. At that time, he also seemed to accept the theory that M. J. Druitt was Jack.

In 1913, Sims wrote a letter to John Littlechild of the Metropolitan Police asking about the Ripper murders. Littlechild had been a chief inspector in 1888 and Sims assumed he had some knowledge of the case. Sims asked if the inspector knew anything about a "Dr. D"—probably referring to Druitt. Littlechild wrote back that he did not, but he offered that "amongst the suspects, and to my mind a very likely one, was a Dr. T. (which sounds much like D). He was an American quack named Francis Tumblety and was at one time a frequent visitor to London and on these occasions constantly brought under the notice of police."[86]

Littlechild said that Tumblety was well known at Scotland Yard and "his feelings toward women were remarkable and bitter in the extreme." At the time of the murders, Tumblety was arrested for other crimes but fled to France before he faced a court. Littlechild wrote that the police believed Tumblety killed himself after this. Whatever happened to him, the Whitechapel murders ended after he left England.

Littlechild's letter survived and turned up for sale in 1993, when Ripperologist Stewart Evans bought it. Evans was a police officer at the time, with an interest in the Ripper case that went back to his childhood. With Littlechild's letter, Evans introduced another name to the list of suspects. The letter also named the journalists the police thought wrote the first Jack the Ripper letter—either Thomas J. Bulling of the Central News Agency or his boss, Charles Moore.

With the name of a new suspect, Evans and others began to

track down all the information they could find about Tumblety. They found a trail of evidence that showed Tumblety passed himself off as a doctor, though he had never been to medical school. He often sold medicines that he claimed could cure the people who came to him, though in one case his pills killed a patient. Tumblety was, as Littlechild called him, a supreme quack—someone who claims he can cure people but is really only after their money.

Tumblety was born in Ireland around 1833 but moved with his family to the United States when he was a boy. After he began his fake medical career, he traveled to various cities in the country and Canada before ending up in Washington, D.C., during the Civil War. In the spring of 1865, he was arrested because he allegedly had ties to a man linked to the assassination of Abraham Lincoln, but he stayed in jail only a few weeks and was not charged with a crime. When he was released, Tumblety wanted to clear his name, so wrote a letter to the *Brooklyn Daily Eagle*, one of the papers that reported his arrest, saying "I have been unconditionally and honorably released from confinement by direction of the Secretary of War, there being no evidence whatever to connect me with the . . . assassination plot, with which some of the Northern journals have charged me of having some knowledge."[87]

A few years after his arrest, Tumblety headed for Europe, visiting London and several other cities. For many years he traveled back and forth between Europe and North America before returning to London in June of 1888. He was arrested for a crime unrelated to the Whitechapel murders and then fled to France, as Inspector Littlechild noted in his letter to George Sims. But Littlechild got one fact wrong: Tumblety did not kill himself soon after. Instead, he went back to New York, perhaps with a London detective trailing him. Ripperologists know that a Scotland Yard detective was in New York at the same time, but there is no proof that he was investigating the Ripper murder or looking for Tumblety.

New York newspapers, however, wrote in December of 1888 that police were looking for Tumblety, possibly because he was a suspect in the Whitechapel murders. New York police were watching for him, since he had fled England before going to court. But as the *New York Times* reported, Chief Inspector Thomas Byrnes of the local police "laughs at the suggestion that he was the Whitechapel murderer or his abettor or accomplice."[88] That statement, however, did not stop the *New York World* several days later from calling Tumblety "the notorious Whitechapel suspect."[89]

Finally, someone—a reporter for the *World*—was able to track down Tumblety. The newspaper published an interview with him on January 29, 1889, and Tumblety gave his theory of why the London police considered him a suspect: "I happened to be there when these Whitechapel murders attracted the attention of the whole world, and, in company with thousands of other people, I went down to the Whitechapel district. I was not dressed in a way to attract attention, I thought, though it afterwards turned out that I did. I was interested by the excitement and the crowds and the queer scenes and sights, and did not know that all the time I was being followed by English detectives. . . . My guilt was very plain to the English mind. Someone had said that Jack the Ripper was an American, and everybody believed that statement. Then it is the universal belief among the lower classes that all Americans wear slouch hats; therefore, Jack the Ripper must wear a slouch hat. Now, I happened to have on a slouch hat, and this, together with the fact that I was an American, was enough for the police. It established my guilt beyond any question."[90]

WAS IT TUMBLETY?

STEWART EVANS AND his cowriter Paul Gainey thought Tumblety was a suspect for another reason besides his nationality and his hat. According to their theory, Tumblety rented a room in the middle of Whitechapel. After the night of the double murders of Catherine Eddowes and Elizabeth Stride, he returned to the room with blood on his shirt. His landlady saw the blood and alerted police, but Tumblety had already left the boarding house and didn't return. Although Tumblety was a prime suspect, the two Ripperologists say, the police did not have evidence to arrest him for the Whitechapel murders. So, they arrested him for his lesser crimes. Interestingly, even though the New York papers asserted that Tumblety was a suspect, the London papers of the time never mentioned his name.

People who suspect Tumblety was Jack offer other reasons

why he could be the killer. In December of 1888, after Tumblety was in New York, a Colonel C. S. Dunham reported having dinner with Tumblety, and the "doctor" talked about how much he hated all women, and especially prostitutes. Dunham, according to a newspaper report, also claimed that Tumblety kept a collection of women's wombs, which filled about a dozen jars.

Dunham's claim tied in to an early rumor in the Ripper murders—that an unnamed American had sought to buy wombs in London. Was Dunham telling the truth about what he'd heard and seen? Had he ever even met Tumblety? No one knows, though one source claims that Dunham was known to be con man; his story could be all lies.

Others who doubt Tumblety was the murderer note that he was close to six feet tall, and one report said he was six foot two. That makes him much taller than the suspects witnesses reported seeing at the times of the murders. Tumblety was also much older than Jack, according to the witnesses. Donald Rumbelow also noted that Tumblety lived until 1903. If the London police had found any convincing evidence against him, they would have tried to arrest him. But that never happened.

To many readers today, the mathematician Charles L. Dodgson is better known as Lewis Carroll, the author of the classic *Alice's Adventures in Wonderland*. Carroll has also made the long list of suspects that some people claim could have been Jack the Ripper. In one of the stranger theories about who Jack might be, Richard Wallace said that Carroll left clues about his crimes in his writing, using anagrams. An anagram is a series of words that can be made from juggling around the letters of other words. So, the phrase "Pat Cipher Jerk" is an anagram of "Jack the Ripper." Wallace, in his book *Jack the Ripper, Light-Hearted Friend*, said the anagrams reveal that Carroll and his friend Thomas Bayne carried out the murders. Karoline Leach, who has studied Carroll's life, said that the anagrams Wallace uses to try to prove Carroll's guilt aren't even anagrams. Wallace leaves out letters or substitutes one for another to create Carroll's "confession." Others have pointed out that Carroll wasn't in London when several of the murders took place. Carroll did make one reference to Jack in his diary. He said that a friend had a theory about Jack's identity. The author, though, did not reveal what the friend's theory was.

THE MERCHANT

ANOTHER CANDIDATE FOR Jack the Ripper also had American ties—through his own murderer. James Maybrick's wife Florence came from a wealthy Alabama family. Maybrick, who bought and sold cotton, met her on a business trip to the United States. In May of 1889, Florence Maybrick made news when she was arrested for killing her husband. Their marriage had begun to fall apart several years before. James was a drug addict and cheated on his wife by sleeping with another woman. Florence then began a relationship with another man. In April of 1889, she began to slowly poison her husband.

James Maybrick wrote about his wife's cheating on him in a diary he kept. In it, he also confessed to being Jack the Ripper. At least that's what some people thought for a time after Michael Barrett of Liverpool, England, published what he said was Maybrick's diary, which contained his confession.

Barrett said that his friend Tony Devereux had given him the book in 1991. Some pages had been ripped out, but among the remaining ones were sixty-three pages filled with handwriting—supposedly Maybrick's. Devereux told Barrett he had found the diary while doing repairs at the Liverpool house Maybrick owned at the time of his death.

In the diary Maybrick gives details about the five murders and another he said he committed in Manchester, England. The diary does not have dates, but the author talks about having "a kidney for supper," which seems to indicate the kidney removed from Catherine Eddowes.[91] At times, though, his details don't match what is known about the killings, such as where some of Mary Kelly's body parts were found. People were quick to call the diary a fake, and after a book about the diary came out in 1993, Barrett admitted that he had forged the book. Soon after, though, he said that his wife, Anne, had forged it. For her part, she said the book had been in her family for decades and she gave it to her husband's friend. She'd wanted her husband to get the book without knowing it came from her family.

Just after *The Diary of Jack the Ripper* was published, another item turned up that supposedly linked Maybrick to the murders. A man named Albert Johnson purchased an old gold watch in Liverpool. Inside, someone had scratched the words, "I am Jack" along with the name J. Maybrick and the initials of Jack's five victims. The timing of the watch's discovery seemed suspicious. Had the diary's forger done this too, to try to give more weight to the idea that Maybrick was Jack?

Since 1992, experts have studied the diary to try to determine if it could be real. The book itself dates to Victorian times. The experts, though, can't say for sure if the ink was from that era. The watch has been analyzed too, to try to date when the scratches were made. While the experts could not say they were recent, they couldn't verify that they dated to 1888, either.

In 1995, Michael Barrett once again asserted that the diary was fake. He said, "The idea of the Diary came from discussion between Tony Devereux, Anne Barrett my wife and myself, there came I time when I believed such a hoax was a distinct possibility. We looked closely at the background of James Maybrick and I read everything to do with the Jack the Ripper matter. I felt Maybrick was an ideal candidate for Jack the Ripper. Most important of all, he could not defend himself. He was not 'Jack the Ripper' of that I am certain, but, times, places, visits to London and all that fitted. It was to (sic) easey (sic). I told my wife Anne Barrett, I said, 'Anne I'll write a best seller here, we can't fail.'"[92]

Despite Barrett's confession, others insisted that Maybrick could still have been Jack the Ripper. Most Ripperologists disagreed. And the hunt to learn Jack's identity continued.

12

THE LASTING FASCINATION WITH JACK THE RIPPER

etectives, real and amateur, have not been the only people fascinated with Jack's story since 1888. His brutal killings and knack for avoiding detection have intrigued writers and other creative people. Some of the earliest stories with Jack as a character appeared in Sweden in 1892. A German playwright used Jack as a character in one of his plays published in 1895, and the story was also turned into an opera. In the play, Jack kills the female lead character.

While some books just called the murderer Jack, others used some of the supposed suspects as characters. And one famous Ripper story drew on a story that circulated in Jack's time. Newspapers reported that police were looking for an unknown lodger at a boarding house who left behind a blood-stained shirt for his landlady to wash, then never returned. In 1889, Dr. Forbes Winslow, who had experience working with the mentally ill, said he had learned that the lodger could be Jack.

The idea of a mentally ill lodger being the killer seemed to spread, because the author Marie Belloc Lowndes used it as the basis of a novel she called *The Lodger*. Lowndes published it 1911 and said she'd gotten the idea for it at a dinner party. She heard one of the guests saying that his parents, who took in lodgers, believed they might have rented a room to Jack the Ripper. In Lowndes's book, an unknown killer called the Avenger is killing prostitutes in London. A couple named Robert and Ellen Bunting have rented a room to a man who arrived carrying a bag and who often goes out late at night—on the same nights when the Avenger has struck. Mrs. Bunting suspects her new lodger is the killer, and she is right, though he escapes without being caught.

The Lodger was not popular at first, but went on to sell hundreds of thousands of copies and was later turned into a play and made into several movies. One of them was a 1927 silent film by director Alfred Hitchcock. He would go on to create some of the most famous mystery and horror films of all time, such as *The Birds* and *Psycho*. In his film of *The Lodger*, he changed the story. The lodger is not a homicidal maniac like Jack the Ripper. He is simply falsely suspected of being one. A talking version of *The Lodger* came out in 1932, called *The Phantom Fiend*. Another was released in 1944, with the lodger once again being the killer, who is definitely meant to be Jack the Ripper. Another film version of the story (also called *The Lodger*) released in 2009, moved the plot to modern-day California, with the murderer simply imitating Jack's crimes.

JACK BY ANOTHER NAME

To some film historians, Alfred Hitchcock's film *The Lodger* was his first classic. He said that he saw a stage version of Marie Belloc Lowndes's story when he was a teen. Decades later, he made another movie that made viewers think of Jack the Ripper: *Frenzy*. In it, a man is falsely accused of carrying out a series of murders against London prostitutes. The actual murderer, though, instead of ripping his victims, strangles them with a necktie. Early in *Frenzy*, a character makes clear the link between this killer and the Whitechapel murderer. He says, "He's a regular Jack the Ripper!"[93] Hitchcock was born in 1899, and he later remembered that mothers would tell their children to behave, or Jack the Ripper would get them.

A POPULAR STORY
TOLD MANY WAYS

SINCE THE FIRST articles and books about Jack the Ripper, more than a thousand books have been written about him, or used the known facts of the case to tell a fictional story. Jack has appeared with other fictional characters, such as Sherlock Holmes, and has supposedly written confessions of his crimes. Jack has also found his way into comic books and graphic novels. He followed Bruce Wayne, better known as Batman, back to Gotham City. He appeared in a graphic novel version of the science fiction TV show *Doctor Who*. Jack was also the "star" of the graphic novel *From Hell*. The title comes from one of the alleged letters Jack wrote during 1888. Starting in 1943, the science fiction writer Robert Bloch wrote several stories featuring Jack the Ripper. In the 1992 novel *Anno Dracula*, Jack lives in a London controlled by vampires.

Some of the stories about Jack have been made into movies, TV shows, and plays. Dozens of films and shows tell the story or use Jack as a character. In the movie *Time After Time*, the author H. G. Wells, who wrote *The Time Machine*, builds a real time machine to track down Jack in the twentieth century. An earlier movie, *A Study in Terror*, pitted Jack against Sherlock Holmes. It was based on a book by the US crime novelist Ellery Queen. Some of the film versions of Jack's story use the theory that Prince Eddy of the royal family was the killer. In several movies, the detective Frederick Abberline is a main character in the hunt to track down Jack. Johnny Depp played Abberline in the film version of *From Hell*.

TV shows that have featured Jack include an episode of the original *Star Trek* show and a TV western. On *Star Trek*, engineer Scotty is suspected of a brutal murder, but the real killer turns out to be Jack. In an episode of *Cimarron Strip*, an Englishman who flees to America begins to commit murder in a small western town. He may or may not be Jack, but the show definitely makes connections to the Ripper murders. In the end, the killer is himself killed by Indians. Harlan Ellison, the science fiction author who wrote that show, turned to Jack's story several times in his work. He said that to him, Jack represented the part of all people who can stand by and watch violence around them without trying to stop it. Jack is a monster, but as Ellison wrote, "We are a culture that needs its monsters."[94]

In Great Britain, the interest in Jack's deeds continued into the twenty-first century. The show *Whitechapel* took the story and moved it into modern times. *Ripper Street* followed the lives of East End detectives after the Ripper murders ended. The first episode featured a murder that was similar to Jack's, but the detectives learn that a new killer is on the loose. Jack and his murders have also been featured in music. Other than its title, the instrumental song "Jack the Ripper" by Link Wray has nothing to do with the Whitechapel murders. Another song with that title, though, does describe Jack and his tale in the lyrics. The 1963 song "Jack the Ripper" starts with the sound of footsteps and heavy breathing, followed by a woman's scream. The words talk about Jack walking the streets at night with his black bag, looking for victims. Screaming Lord Sutch, who recorded that song in 1963, pretended to be Jack when he sang it live. He "stabbed" the other musicians onstage and threw animal hearts and livers into the crowd. "Jack the Ripper" is also the name of a song by the rapper LL Cool J, though the lyrics don't talk about the murderer and his crimes.

Jack has even found his way into video games. One once again features Jack in a battle of wits with Sherlock Holmes. Another game is set in New York, and a journalist is trying to track down a murderer whose crimes are similar to Jack's. The killer turns out to be Jack himself. Jack and his murders have also been the subject of exhibits at Madame Tussaud's, a famous wax museum in London. (Several of the museums are now also open in other countries, including the United States.) The museum's Chamber of Horrors once had wax images of some of the suspects linked to the Ripper murders, such as George Chapman. The museum, though, has never created a Jack the Ripper statue since no one knows what he looks like, and the museum only shows the likeness of real, known people. An 1980 exhibit at Madame Tussaud's did show several of Jack's victims and recreated the Ten Bells pub, where victim Mary Kelly drank the night of her murder. (For a time in the 1970s and '80s the real pub was renamed for Jack, though today it is once again the Ten Bells.)

Why have so many artists chosen to tell Jack's tale in so many ways? Part of it might be because there are so many mysteries about the case: Who was Jack, and how did he get away with murder? Part of it may be people's fascination with horror stories. As Ellison wrote, we all need monsters, which can represent the evil we sometimes see in ourselves. And with Jack's identity unknown, a creative writer can make him anyone they want him to be. One writer, instead of making Jack battle Sherlock Holmes, wrote a story in which Holmes is actually the killer!

THE OTHER RIPPERS

In modern times, the phrase "serial killer" is used to describe someone like Jack. A serial killer typically kills a number of people, following a pattern in how he (most are men) chooses victims and carries out the murder. Law enforcement officials have come up with several definitions of who is a serial killer. In general, it's someone who kills at least two people in different locations, taking time after one murder before striking again. Often, there is a sexual element—the killer somehow connects the sexual act with violence.

THE FBI AND JACK THE RIPPER

The Federal Bureau of Investigation has created profiles of people who carry out violent crimes. The profiles describe the traits of a likely suspect. In 1988, an FBI investigator named John Douglas described the type of suspect the FBI would look for if it were hunting for Jack the Ripper. The killer, Douglas said, committed what the FBI calls lust murders—

in these murders, the killer targets a victim's sexual organs. Douglas said Jack was white, as lust murderers usually target victims of their own race. He most likely would have been between 28 and 36 years old, but the FBI would not rule out younger or older suspects. He probably dressed well on the night of the killings, so the prostitutes would assume he had money and approach him first. A lust killer like Jack would probably not be married and have few close friends. Douglas said it is likely that Jack lived in the Whitechapel area and may even have been questioned by the police. And Jack most likely did not commit suicide, as suspect M. J. Druitt did. Douglas wrote, "Generally, when crimes such as these cease, it is because [the killer] came close to being identified, was interviewed by the police, or was arrested for some other type of offense."[95]

Jack was not the first known serial killer, just the first one to receive international attention. Jack may also have been the first serial killer to share information about his crimes with the police, if the "From Hell" letter that came with part of a kidney was really from him. Given the fame of the Ripper murders, some serial killers after Jack were sometimes labeled Rippers too, showing his lasting influence.

One of these later serial killers was Peter Kurten. A resident of Düsseldorf, Germany, Kurten claimed that when he was nine, he killed two boys by throwing them in a river and holding them under the water. As a teen, he was arrested for stealing and spent time in prison. There, he said, he read about Jack the Ripper. He later said, "I thought what pleasure it would give me to do things of that kind once I got out again."[96] Years passed before Kurten began his own killing spree in Düsseldorf.

Starting in 1925, Kurten tried to strangle several women. In 1929 he almost murdered one by stabbing her repeatedly with scissors. Into 1930 he carried out a series of attacks, sometimes stabbing his victims, sometimes strangling them or beating them with a hammer. Unlike Jack, Kurten didn't always manage to kill his subjects, and at times he attacked men. But to many newspapers, Kurten became the "Düsseldorf Ripper." Kurten reinforced the link to Jack when he sent a letter to the police, telling them where they could find the bodies of several victims.

As in London, Düsseldorf and Berlin police conducted a huge hunt for the killer. Kurten finally turned himself in and confessed to his crimes. He explained the pleasure he got killing both people and animals. Kurten was found guilty of nine murders and executed in 1931.

Another serial killer who earned the nickname Ripper was Peter Sutcliffe. Starting in 1975 and continuing for five years, Sutcliffe killed at least thirteen women and tried to kill more in Yorkshire and other parts of England. Because some of the victims were prostitutes and because of the way he sliced up some of the victims, Sutcliffe was called the Yorkshire Ripper. The police also received several letters and an audio tape from someone claiming to the be the killer, just as with the Whitechapel murders and the Düsseldorf Ripper. The sender signed the letters "Jack the Ripper." But these messages turned out to be hoaxes.

The police questioned Sutcliffe several times about the murders before he was caught. He was found guilty and sent to a psychiatric hospital. In 2015 British newspapers reported that this Ripper might have been responsible for even more killings than the ones he was arrested for—as many as twenty-two more.

The Rippers that followed Jack also stirred up great fear. But unlike him, history knows who they were. Jack's identity remains a mystery.

13

JACK FOUND AT LAST?

The search to find out Jack's identity has continued into the twenty-first century and shows no signs of slowing down. As with the DNA testing of Catherine Eddowes's shawl, described in chapter 10, sometimes investigators call on modern science to try to pin Jack down. Other times people claim to find new evidence that reveals who he was. And since books about Jack are still popular, some writers assure the public that their versions of events solve the mystery once and for all.

That was the case with Patricia Cornwell, who called her 2002 book about Jack *Portrait of a Killer: Jack the Ripper—Case Closed*. Cornwell, an American author of crime novels, said Jack was someone who had been linked to the case decades before: the artist Walter Sickert. He was one of the men who supposedly helped royal doctor Sir William Gull kill Mary Kelly and the others after Prince Eddy secretly married and fathered a child.

In Cornwell's version of events, Sickert was Jack and acted alone, and he might have carried out killings in France as well. For evidence, Cornwell first poured through hundreds of the false Ripper letters police received in 1888. She compared a type of DNA known as mitochondrial DNA found on some of them with DNA found on letters that Sickert definitely wrote. The DNA matched, but once again skeptics raised several issues. The DNA on both samples could have been contaminated, and thousands of people in England at the time could have had the same DNA as the kind found on the Ripper letters. Still, Cornwell believed that Sickert wrote many of the letters, often disguising his handwriting. Of course, even if Sickert wrote some of the letters, that does not mean he was Jack. Many people claimed to be Jack, but their letters were hoaxes.

Cornwell also looked at visual evidence Sickert left behind. He was an artist, and he did a series of paintings called *The Camden Town Murder*. He painted them after a prostitute named Emily Dimmock was killed in 1907, with her throat slit. Cornwell says the scenes in some of the paintings are similar to murder scenes of several of Jack's victims. But knowing the details of the Mary Kelly death scene, for example, does not mean Sickert was there to see it. A picture of that scene was published in France in 1899, and Sickert often visited there. Plus, a medical magazine called the *Lancet* sometimes had detailed descriptions of the crime scenes.

Sickert does seem to have had an interest in Jack the Ripper. After renting one room, Sickert learned from his landlady that a student who once lived in the house had been Jack the Ripper. Sickert then painted his room and called it *Jack the Ripper's Room*. But many artists of different kinds were interested in Jack during that time. Crime and people living outside of "respectable" society often turned up in art and literature. To Ripperologists, Cornwell did not close the case on Jack's identity.

MORE POSSIBILITIES

IN 2011 A Spanish writer named José Luis Abad y Benítez raised the possibility that a person with deep ties to the Ripper murder could be Jack. Abad, who said he was an expert in studying hand-writing, said Inspector Frederick Abberline was the killer! Abad said that not only was the Maybrick diary found in Liverpool real, but that Abberline, not James Maybrick, had written it. While Abad's claim made some London newspapers, few people seemed to take it seriously.

The same year another suspect's name made the papers: Carl Feigenbaum. He was a German sailor who was executed in the United States in 1896 for killing his landlady. Sailors had some-times turned up as suspects in 1888. Ships docked near White-chapel along the Thames River. Sailors visited East End pubs and sought out prostitutes. It would have been easy for a sailor Jack to flee London after each crime as he set off on a new voyage. But while a television show featured Feigenbaum in 2011, he had been mentioned as a suspect before. Retired police detective

Trevor Marriott had named him as Jack in his 2005 book, *Jack the Ripper: The 21st Century Investigation*. Feigenbaum's name, though, had come up long before that.

Right after Feigenbaum was executed, his lawyer William Lawton spoke to a New York newspaper. Lawton said, "I believe that Carl Feigenbaum, whom you have just seen put to death in the electric chair, can easily be connected with the Jack-the-Ripper murders in Whitechapel, London. . . . I will stake my professional reputation that if the police will trace this man's movements carefully for the last few years, their investigations will lead them to London and to Whitechapel." Lawton based his comments on what Feigenbaum had told him before his death. The lawyer said his client told him that that he suffered from a disease that drove him "to kill and mutilate every woman who falls in my way. At such times I am unable to control myself."[97]

Ripperologist Marriott had thought for several years that Jack was a sailor who often docked in London. He focused on German ships and found one that was in port on the day of several of the killings. Marriott then looked at the crew list and, using Lawton's statement, named Feigenbaum as the killer.

Marriott also found killings that occurred in other countries after the Ripper murders and while Feigenbaum was still working as a sailor. Among other theories Marriott introduced in his book, he said Jack did not steal the body parts missing from the murder victims. Instead, Marriott wrote, someone stole them after the murder and before the medical examinations.

Experts who doubt Feigenbaum was Jack point to several facts. Lawton was not the only lawyer who represented Feigenbaum in New York. The other, Hugh Pentecost, thought the German was guilty but did not believe he was Jack. And during the trial Lawton never shared with him Feigenbaum's supposed confession. As far as other murders Feigenbaum might have committed, no one has proof that he was in those countries when the murders took place.

THE SECRET RIPPER FILES

After completing research for his 2005 book, Trevor Marriott continued to search police files for clues about Jack the Ripper. In 2008 he learned that Scotland Yard had kept secret four books that contained information about the case.

Some of the records referred to informants who had given the police the names of possible suspects in the Whitechapel murders. Marriott believed the records also named four men who could have been Jack the Ripper. When he asked to see the records, Scotland Yard said no. It argued that revealing the names of informants, even ones who died decades ago, might make twenty-first century informants less likely to help the police. They might fear that the police would one day reveal their names. If criminals found out, they might go after the informants' living relatives. Marriott took the police to court. At one point a Scotland Yard official known only as Detective Inspector D spoke from behind a curtain to keep his identity a secret. He repeated the police's arguments against revealing the information, saying, "Confidence in the system is maintaining the safety of informants, regardless of age."[98] The court ruled against Marriott and said the records should remain secret. Marriott believed that revealing the contents of the records may have helped identify Jack once and for all.

A HUSBAND AND A KILLER

IN 2015 A new name emerged as a suspect in the Ripper murders: Francis Spurzheim Craig, a reporter who lived in the East End. The man who made the claim was Dr. Wynne Weston-Davies, who said that he was related to Jack's last victim, Mary Kelly. Yet Weston-Davies insisted that her real identity was Elizabeth Weston-Davies, and that she had been married to Craig. Dr. Weston-Davies also said that Elizabeth was his great aunt, a claim he wanted to verify by exhuming the body of Mary Kelly and having a DNA test done to show they were related.

Weston-Davies, like most Ripperologists, outlined his claim in a book, *The Real Mary Kelly*. He said that in researching his family history, he learned the connection between his great aunt and Francis Craig. Their marriage didn't last after Elizabeth turned to prostitution. An angry Craig wanted to kill her, but first he murdered the other four women and created the killer Jack the Ripper to cover his final crime. Dr. Weston-Davies believed that Craig, not Thomas Bulling, wrote the "Dear Boss" letter in which Jack's name first appeared.

Weston-Davies said he was stunned to learn about how Craig died: "I realized he had committed suicide by slitting his own throat with a blade, exactly the same way the Ripper's victims had been murdered"[99]

Weston-Davies believes that Craig badly mutilated Kelly so no one would ever identify her as his former wife. Elizabeth, for her part, changed her name to Mary Kelly to make it harder for Craig to track her down, which he did several years after their divorce. To prove his relation to Elizabeth and that his theory is right, Weston-Davies convinced the British government to allow his great aunt's body to be dug up so the DNA test could be performed. Other people had made similar requests for Jack's victims, but Weston-Davies was the first to receive permission, though the government placed conditions on this. As of 2016, the test had not been performed. Still, showing a family link between Weston-Davies and the person who was known as Mary Kelly would not prove that Francis Craig was Jack the Ripper. But it might be one step in that process.

ANOTHER MAYBRICK

AT ALMOST THE same time that Weston-Davies presented his theory, Bruce Robinson published his explanation of who Jack was. In *They All Loved Jack: Busting the Ripper*, Robinson goes back to an old theory—that the killings were carried out by a Freemason, and other Freemasons knew his identity. The Freemasons are also known as Masons, and their organization still exists today. They trace their roots to a social group that formed in England hundreds of years ago. The Freemasons used secret handshakes and passwords to identify one another, which over the years has led some people to assume their group is a "secret society." The Freemasons have also attracted many business and government leaders as members.

The earlier theory that Prince Eddy and Sir William Gull had ties to the Ripper murder also included the role of Freemasons. Gull and the government official who supposedly ordered the killing of Mary Kelly were Freemasons. So was Sir Charles Warren, the Metropolitan Police commissioner in 1888.

According to Robinson, he ordered that the famous "the Juwes are the men . . ." graffiti be washed off a wall because he knew it related to Masonic teachings. He assumed whoever wrote it was also a Mason, and Warren wanted to protect another member of the society. Robinson rejects the explanation that Warren gave at the time for erasing the graffiti: that he wanted to prevent a rise in anti-Semitic violence.

No serious Ripperologists accepts the idea that the royal family had ties to the Whitechapel murders. Most have rejected the idea of a Masonic conspiracy. But in a book more than eight hundred pages long, Robinson argues that the Freemasons did take part in a conspiracy, and that Jack was a Mason named Michael Maybrick—the brother of James Maybrick, an earlier Ripper suspect.

Thanks to fifteen years of research, Robinson learned that Sir Charles Warren was not just a Mason. He was actively involved in the organization, and Robinson thinks that he did not want Jack to be identified. Other people involved investigating the case, including Chief Inspector Donald Swanson and coroner Wynne Baxter, were also Freemasons. Robinson said in 2015,

"They weren't protecting Jack the Ripper, they were protecting the system [of Freemasonry] that Jack the Ripper was threatening. And to protect the system, they had to protect him. And Jack knew it."[100]

Robinson's research led him to read the James Maybrick diary, which most people think is a hoax. Robinson, though, thought it was real, and that James's brother Michael wrote it. He was a popular singer and songwriter of the Victorian era. Robinson said he wrote many of the Jack letters, leaving clues to his identity and ties to Freemasonry. Postmarks on the letters match the dates and places Maybrick visited while on tour, performing across England. No murders took place when Maybrick was far from London.

———◆———

THE MYSTERY CONTINUES

ROBINSON CALLED HIS book "an argument . . . with all these self-appointed experts—these Ripperologists."[101] He was convinced that he had found Jack the Ripper at last. Some people will try to disprove his theory, while others might look for more evidence to support it. Maybe the true identity of Jack will finally be known—or not. Someone else is bound to come forward with what he or she claims is new evidence that proves who Jack was.

Many people fascinated with the Whitechapel murders say they want to discover the truth about Jack. But will finding out his identity end his appeal? Today, visitors to London can go to a Jack the Ripper Museum or take the tours in Whitechapel of Ripper sites. Would people stop being Ripper tourists if they knew he was really an angry journalist or a famous singer?

Not knowing who Jack really was creates a sense of mystery that people enjoy. And it's not just the mystery that attracts us. Ripperologist Paul Begg thinks there is something else about Jack that draws our attention. To most people, Begg said, Jack represents "the fear that we all have of the lurker in the shadows, that thing we can offer no defense against."[102] If Jack's identity is discovered, people may look for another symbol of that universal human fear.

ACKNOWLEDGMENTS

I would like to thank the many dedicated amateur and professional students of Jack the Ripper and his murders, in particular the many people who have made the Casebook: Jack the Ripper website such a valuable collection of primary sources for information on the investigations, the victims, and the suspects. I could not have written as detailed a book as this without those sources.

TIME LINE

June 28, 1887	Miriam Angel's body is found.
August 21, 1887	Israel Lipski hangs for the murder of Miriam Angel.
March 10, 1888	Michael Ostrog is released from an insane asylum.
August 7, 1888	Martha Tabram's body is found in George Yard.
August 31, 1888	Mary Ann Nichols's body is found in Buck's Row.
September 5, 1888	The Star publishes a write-up on John Pizer, also known as "Leather Apron."
September 8, 1888	Annie Chapman's body is found at 29 Hanbury Street.
September 10, 1888	John Pizer is arrested.
September 29, 1888	The Central News Agency receives the "Dear Boss" letter from Jack the Ripper.

September 30, 1888	Elizabeth Stride's body is found on Berner Street.
	Catherine Eddowes's body is found in Mitre Square.
October 1, 1888	The Central News Agency receives a postcard from Jack the Ripper.
October 16, 1888	George Lusk receives a package containing half a human kidney.
November 7, 1888	Francis Tumblety is arrested.
November 9, 1888	Mary Kelly's body is found at 26 Dorset Street.
November 24, 1888	Francis Tumblety flees to France.
November 30, 1888	Montague Druitt's employer fires him.
December 31, 1888	Montague Druitt's body is found in the River Thames.
May 11, 1889	James Maybrick dies.
July 17, 1889	Alice McKenzie's body is found in Castle Alley.

February 7, 1891	Aaron Kosminski is transferred to Colney Hatch.
February 13, 1891	Frances Coles's body is found in Swallow Gardens.
March 5, 1891	Thomas Cutbush is sent to Lambeth Infirmary for lunacy.
March 19, 1903	George Chapman is convicted of murder.
April 7, 1903	George Chapman hangs.
September 23, 1913	Chief Inspector John Littlechild writes the Littlechild letter to George Sims.

NOTES

1. Philip Sugden, *The Complete History of Jack the Ripper* (London: Robinson, 2002), 45.

2. Sugden, *Complete History*, 35.

3. http://www.casebook.org/official_documents/inquests/inquest_nichols.html.

4. http://www.casebook.org/witnesses/w/John_Thain.html.

5. http://www.casebook.org/press_reports/daily_news/18880901.html.

6. http://www.casebook.org/press_reports/daily_news/18880901.html.

7. http://www.casebook.org/press_reports/new_york_times/nyt880901.html.

8. http://www.casebook.org/official_documents/inquests/inquest_nichols.html.

9. Ibid.

10. Ibid.

11. Richard Jones, *Jack the Ripper: The Casebook*, (London: Andre Deutsch, 2012), 6.

12. Jones, *Casebook*, 7.

13. http://www.victorianweb.org; http://www.victorianweb.org/history/slums.html.

14. http://www.casebook.org/press_reports/east_london_advertiser/ela880811.html.

15. http://www.casebook.org/press_reports/east_london_advertiser/ela880908.html.

16. http://www.telegraph.co.uk/travel/destinations/europe/uk/london/11123209
    /Are-Jack-the-Ripper-tours-blighting-London.html.

17. Sugden, *Complete History*, 73.

18. Jones, *Casebook*, 21.

19. http://www.casebook.org/press_reports/east_london_advertiser/ela880908.html.

20. http://www.casebook.org/official_documents/inquests/inquest_chapman.html.

21. Donald Rumbelow, *The Complete Jack the Ripper*, (London: Virgin Books, 2013) 35.

22. Sugden, *Complete History*, 85.

23. http://www.casebook.org/official_documents/inquests/inquest_chapman.html.

24. Sugden, *Complete History*, 86.

25. Sugden, *Complete History*, 91.

26. http://www.casebook.org/ripper_media/rps.walterdew.html.

27. Sugden, *Complete History*, 124.

28. http://www.casebook.org/press_reports/east_london_advertiser/ela880929.html.

29. http://www.casebook.org/press_reports/pall_mall_gazette/18880924.html.

30. Paul Begg, *Jack the Ripper: The Definitive History*, (London: Routledge, 2004), 89.

31. http://www.casebook.org/witnesses/w/J._Best.html.

32. http://www.casebook.org/official_documents/inquests/inquest_stride.html.

33. Sugden, *Complete History*, 201-202.

34. http://www.casebook.org/press_reports/star/s881001.html.

35. Sugden, *Complete History*, 221.

36. http://www.casebook.org/press_reports/star/s881003.html.

37. http://www.casebook.org/official_documents/inquests/inquest_eddowes.html.

38. http://www.casebook.org/press_reports/star/s881001.html.

39. http://www.casebook.org/official_documents/inquests/inquest_eddowes.html.

40. http://www.casebook.org/official_documents/inquests/inquest_eddowes.html.

41. http://www.casebook.org/press_reports/daily_news/18881001.html.

42. Jones, *Casebook*, 28.

43. Sugden, *Complete History*, 186.

44. http://casebook.org/dissertations/rip-wallwriting.html.

45. http://www.casebook.org/press_reports/star/s881003.html.

46. http://www.casebook.org/press_reports/east_london_advertiser/ela881013.html.

47. Rumbelow, *Complete Jack*, 109.

48. Sugden, *Complete History*, 263.

49. http://www.casebook.org/press_reports/times/18881008.html.

50. Sugden, *Complete History*, 328.

51. Rumbelow, *Complete Jack*, 101.

52. http://www.casebook.org/witnesses/w/George_Hutchinson.html.

53. http://www.casebook.org/witnesses/w/Thomas_Bowyer.html.

54. Sugden, *Complete History*, 313.

55. Sugden, *Complete History*, 320.

56. Sugden, *Complete History*, 316.

57. http://www.casebook.org/press_reports/daily_news/18881110.html.

58. http://www.casebook.org/official_documents/inquests/inquest_kelly.html.

59. https://books.google.com/books (The Spectator, Volume 61) https://books.google.com/books?id=BO0hAQAAMAAJ&pg=PA1581&lpg=PA1581&dq=sir+charles+warren+resignation&source=bl&ots=HrvjzzHO6n&sig=aN0lmsAZMQ3wVGjHt1Iuj85dXhk&hl=en&sa=X&ved=0ahUKEwjP8vSi18rKAhUJ9WMKHcsFAgwQ6AEISzAL#v=onepage&q=sir%20charles%20warren%20resignation%20whitechapel&f=false.

60. http://www.casebook.org/press_reports/new_york_world/18881111.html.

61. http://www.casebook.org/victims/mckenzie.html.

62. Ibid.

63. http://www.casebook.org/press_reports/east_london_advertiser/ela910214.html.

64. Begg, *Definitive History*, 221.

65. Rumbelow, *Complete Jack,* 144.

66. http://www.casebook.org/press_reports/pall_mall_gazette/18891104.html.

67. Ibid.

68. Ibid.

69. Ibid.

70. Jones, *Casebook*, 56.

71. http://www.casebook.org/press_reports/sun/18940216.html.

72. Rumbelow, *Complete Jack,* 144.

73. http://www.casebook.org/suspects/druitt.html.

74. Ibid.

75. Sugden, *Complete History*, 385.

76. http://www.casebook.org/press_reports/pall_mall_gazette/19030331.html.

77. Sugden, *Complete History*, 398-399.

78. Ibid.

79. http://www.casebook.org/press_reports/pall_mall_gazette/19030324.html.

80. http://www.casebook.org/press_reports/pall_mall_gazette/19030331.html.

81. Sugden, *Complete History*, 450.

82. Sugden, *Complete History*, 208.

83. http://www.casebook.org/dissertations/maybrick_diary/mb-mc.html.

84. http://www.casebook.org/press_reports/evening_news/18881016.html.

85. Sugden, *Complete History*, 8.

86. http://www.casebook.org/official_documents/lcletter.html.

87. http://www.casebook.org/official_documents/lcletter.html.

88. http://www.casebook.org/press_reports/new_york_times/nyt881204.html.

89. http://www.casebook.org/press_reports/new_york_world/18881206.html.

90. http://www.casebook.org/dissertations/rip-slouch.html.

91. http://www.jamesmaybrick.org/pdf%20files/Diary%20(William%20Beadle%20article).pdf.

92. http://www.casebook.org/suspects/james_maybrick/mb-con.bjan5.html.

93. http://www.stephenvolk.net/Alfred.pdf.

94. Ellen Weil and Gary K. Wolfe, *Harlan Ellison: The Edge of Forever*, (Columbus: Ohio State University Press, 2002), 117.

95. https://vault.fbi.gov/Jack%20the%20Ripper/Jack%20the%20Ripper%20Part%201%20of%201/view.

96. Rumbelow, *Complete Jack,* 319.

97. http://www.casebook.org/suspects/carl-feigenbaum.html.

98. http://www.telegraph.co.uk/news/uknews/crime/8514000/Scotland-Yard-fights-to
-keep-Jack-the-Ripper-files-secret.html.

99. http://www.telegraph.co.uk/news/uknews/crime/11771381/Jack-the-Ripper-identity
-mystery-solved-in-new-book.html.

100. http://www.telegraph.co.uk/news/uknews/crime/11899901/jack-the
-ripper-mystery-solved.html.

101. Ibid.

102. http://news.bbc.co.uk/2/hi/uk_news/4042087.stm.

GLOSSARY

ACCOMPLICE: Someone who helps someone else, particularly in committing a crime

ARISTOCRAT: A person from a noble family, who can pass down a title such as "Lord" or "Baron"

COMMISSIONER: The person in charge of certain government agencies

CONSTABLE: A British police officer

EXHUMED: Dug up after it was buried

HOMICIDAL: Likely to commit a homicide, another word for murder

INSPECTOR: A police officer usually ranking next below a superintendent

MEMBRANE: A thin, flexible covering, particularly in a living organism

MORTUARY: Place where dead bodies are taken before burial

MOTIVE: The reason for doing something, such as committing a crime

VIGILANCE: Careful watch over something

FURTHER READING

BOOKS

Anderson, Jennifer Joline. *Jack the Ripper*. Minneapolis, MN: ABDO Publishing, 2012.

Jones, Richard. *Jack the Ripper: The Casebook*. London: Andre Deutsch, 2012.

Kramer, Ann. *Victorians*. London: Dorling Kindersley, 2015.

Olson, Kay Melchisedech. *Murderers and Serial Killers: Stories of Violent Criminals*. Mankato, MN: Capstone Press, 2010.

WEBSITES

CASEBOOK: JACK THE RIPPER http://www.casebook.org/

JACK THE RIPPER http://www.bbc.co.uk/history/historic_figures/ripper_jack_the.shtml

JACK THE RIPPER AND THE EAST END http://www.museumoflondon.org.uk/explore-online/pocket-histories/jack-ripper-and-east-end/

JACK THE RIPPER MUSEUM http://www.jacktherippermuseum.com/

JACK THE RIPPER TOUR http://www.jack-the-ripper-walk.co.uk/

SELECT BIBLIOGRAPHY

Begg, Paul. *Jack the Ripper: The Definitive History*. London: Routledge, 2004.

Begg, Paul, and John Bennett. *Jack the Ripper: The Forgotten Victims*. New Haven: Yale University Press, 2013.

Corton, Christine L. *London Fog: The Biography*. Cambridge: Belknap Press, 2015.

Harrison, Shirley. *The Diary of Jack the Ripper: The Chilling Confession of James Maybrick*. London: John Blake Publishing, 2010.

Jones, Richard. *Jack the Ripper: The Casebook*. London: Andre Deutsch, 2012.

Ramsland, Katherine. *Inside the Minds of Serial Killers*. Westport, CT: Praeger, 2006.

Rumbelow, Donald. *The Complete Jack the Ripper*. London: Virgin Books, 2013.

Sugden, Philip. *The Complete History of Jack the Ripper*. London: Robinson Publishing, 2006.

Weil, Ellen, and Gary K. Wolfe. *Harlan Ellison: The Edge of Forever*. Columbus: Ohio State University Press, 2002.

WEBSITES

Bennett, John. "A Look at the Ripper Centenary in 1988." MADAME GUILLOTINE. http://madameguillotine.org.uk/2012/10/04/a-look-at-the-ripper-centenary-in-1988-by-john-bennett/

CASEBOOK: JACK THE RIPPER. http://www.casebook.org/

FBI RECORDS: JACK THE RIPPER. https://vault.fbi.gov/Jack%20the%20 Ripper/Jack%20the%20Ripper%20Part%201%20of%201/view

MENTAL HEALTH AND ILLNESS. SCIENCE MUSEUM. http://www .sciencemuseum.org.uk/broughttolife/themes/menalhealthandillness

THE VICTORIAN WEB. http://www.victorianweb.org/index.html

ABOUT THE AUTHOR

Michael Burgan has written more than 250 books for children and young adults, both fiction and nonfiction. His works include biographies of US and world leaders and histories of the American Revolution, World War II, and the Cold War. A graduate of the University of Connecticut with a degree in history, Burgan is also a produced playwright and the editor of *The Biographer's Craft*, the newsletter of Biographers International Organization. He lives in Santa Fe, New Mexico, with his cat, Callie.

Looking for another great book?
Find it
IN THE MIDDLE.

Fun, fantastic books for kids
in the in-be**TWEEN** age.

IntheMiddleBooks.com

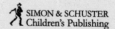